JOHNSTON PUBLIC LIBRARY
IJOH 00 0 074739 M

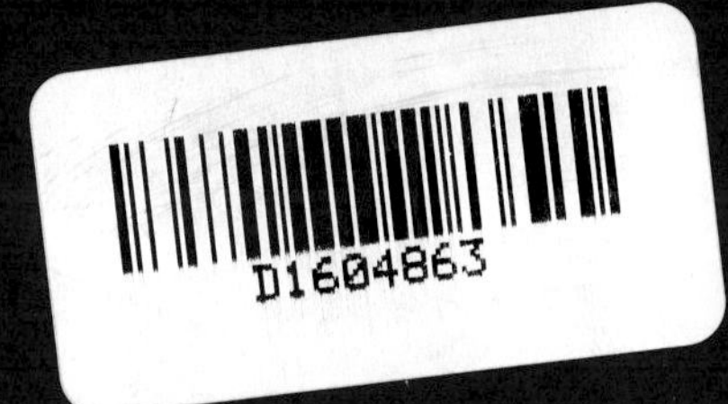
D1604863

THE WAY OF THE NINJA

THE WAY OF THE NINJA

Secret Techniques

Masaaki Hatsumi

TRANSLATED BY Ben Jones

KODANSHA INTERNATIONAL
Tokyo · New York · London

NOTE FROM THE PUBLISHER:
This book is presented only as a means of preserving a unique aspect of the heritage of the martial arts. Neither the publisher nor the author makes any representation, warranty, or guarantee that the techniques described or illustrated in it will be safe or effective in any self-defense situation or otherwise. Readers may be injured if they apply or train in the techniques illustrated. To minimize the risk of injury, nothing described in this book should be undertaken without personal and expert instruction. In addition, a physician should be consulted before deciding whether or not to attempt any of the techniques described. Federal, state, or local law may prohibit the use or the possession of any of the weapons described or illustrated in this book. Specific self-defense responses illustrated there may not be justified in any particular situation or under applicable federal, state, or local law. Neither the publisher nor the author makes any representation or warranty regarding the legality or appropriateness of any weapon or technique mentioned in this book.

Jacket photos and most step-by-step photos by Kyuzo Akashi; some step-by-step photos by Tomoaki Sasaki.

Distributed in the United States by Kodansha America, Inc., and in the United Kingdom and continental Europe by Kodansha Europe Ltd.

Published by Kodansha International Ltd., 17-14 Otowa 1-chome, Bunkyo-ku, Tokyo 112-8652, and Kodansha America, Inc.

ISBN 4-7700-2805-9

First edition, 2004
10 09 08 07 06 05 04   10 9 8 7 6 5 4 3 2

www.kodansha-intl.com

Single-minded perseverance (Picture by the author)

忍法一貫

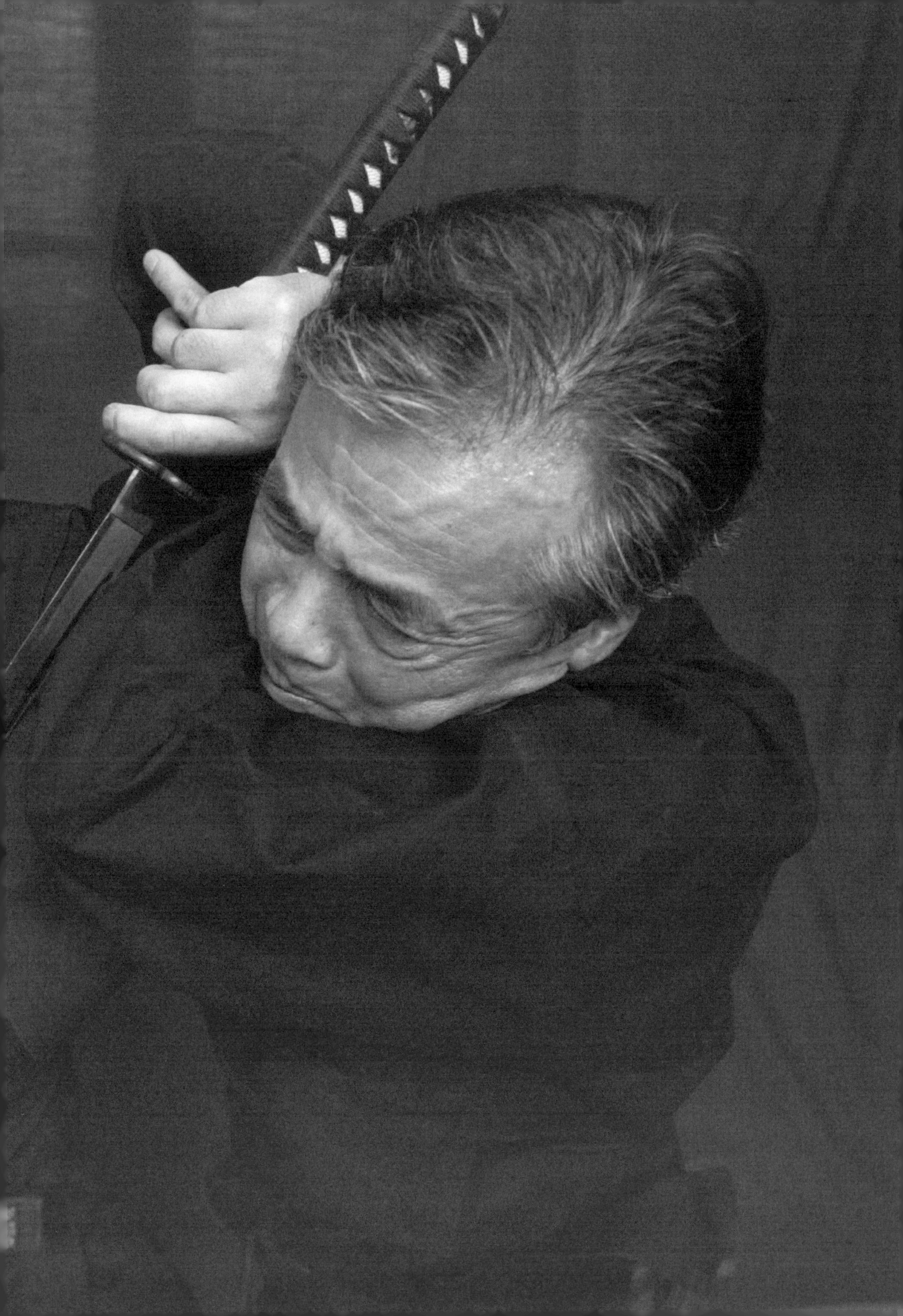

CONTENTS

Emperor Jimmu, with the golden kite who dazzled his enemies and granted him victory. The calligraphy says "Butoku Ikō": martial virtue shines out.

Chapter

1

Ninjutsu, a Japanese art

日本文化としての忍術

THE WAY OF WAR IS SURVIVAL

What made you choose this book? Was it some desire to learn 'winning' techniques? If so, there is something I have to tell you: in the long run, those who focus on winning inevitably taste the bitterness of defeat. The important thing in the martial arts is not to win—it is to survive. The most vital techniques in Budō are those which preserve life. That is why the ultimate secret of the martial arts is said to be "to win without fighting." It is my sincere hope, therefore, that this book will help you to understand two major principles. One is that Ninjutsu is the very backbone of the martial arts; the other, that Ninjutsu shows us the true, divine intent of the martial arts.

The martial arts were born shrouded in mystery out of bare-handed body arts (Taijutsu) based on the core concepts of Ninpō. As time went on, recognizable 'forms' or ways of using sticks, swords, spears and the like gradually developed. At the same time, the martial arts became a valuable repository of eternal truths, almost like a wind of wisdom blowing across the pages of history, conjured up through the training and self-sacrifice of countless individuals.

I should like to begin my account of Budō by introducing you to a document written by my lifelong teacher, Takamatsu Toshitsugu, 33rd Grandmaster of the Togakure School. Its title is "Precepts of Perseverance in the Martial Ways," and it contains a set of guiding principles drawn up by the 32nd Grandmaster, Toda Shinryūken. In just five articles, it manages to encompass the essence of Budō and of Ninjutsu.

- Learn first that whatever hardship you may have to endure is but temporary
- Always behave correctly
- Do not fall prey to avarice, indulgence, or egoism
- Sorrow and hate are both part of life; understand that they too are gifts from the gods
- Never stray from the path of the spirit, nor that of the martial arts; be ambitious in the ways of both pen and sword

A Ninja was someone whose very existence expressed the spirit of Budō. He would protect himself with techniques not of assassination but rather of sensation and awareness. He would avoid unnecessary conflict, and even if armed with a blade, would find a

Takamatsu Toshitsugu Sensei

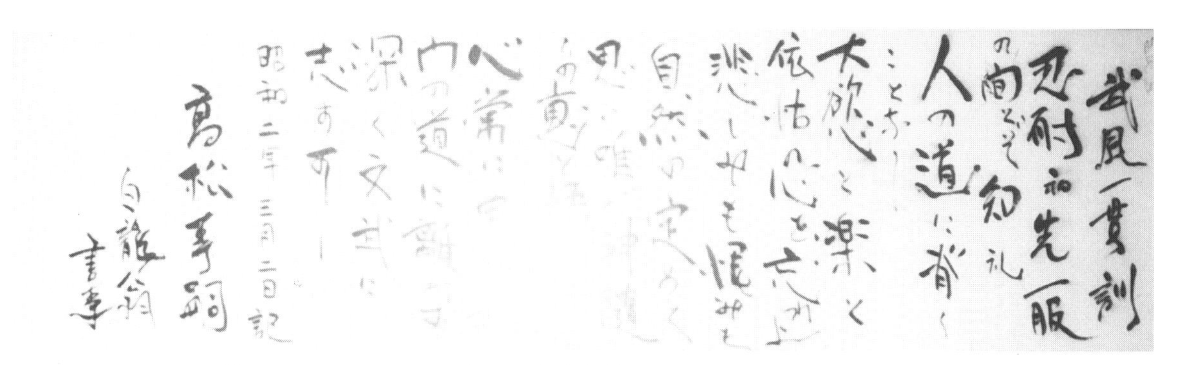

"Precepts of Perseverance in the Martial Ways"

A Makimono scroll from the author's teacher, inscribed "Takamatsu Toshitsugu Kikaku proclaims Hatsumi Masaaki to be Sōke"

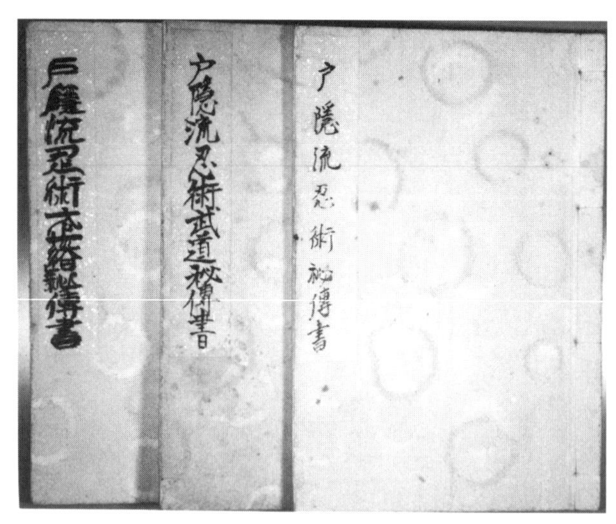

Hidensho—documents of the secrets of Togakure-ryū Ninjutsu Budō, transmitted to the author by Takamatsu Sensei

way to win without staining it. These are the true techniques of Ninjutsu. This is the art in which Ninja trained, persistently, throughout their lives. After crushing Napoleon's resurgence at Waterloo, the great British general Wellington (1769–1852) said, "Next to a battle lost, the greatest misery is a battle gained." He evidently understood that the secret of happiness is not to fight at all.

A Ninja's costume is known as "Ninniku Yoroi"—Ninniku Armor. Ninniku literally means 'forbearance,' and also refers to a Buddhist monk's robes. The spirit of the Ninja is thus based on the principle of bearing insults and swallowing the desire for revenge. In other words, the fundamental rule of the Ninja when faced with an enemy's attack is to evade it naturally and disappear, using Ninpō Taijutsu (concealment skills sometimes referred to as "Tongyō no Jutsu"). Only when no other option is left open would a Ninja make use of natural principles and methods to fell his opponent.

Ninja did not value survival because of a fear of death. They exercised endurance throughout their secretive lives in order to protect their families, their clans, and their country. Their harsh training endowed them with a tough but pliant spirit and martial skills suitable for coping with any situation, together with a sense of awareness that had universal application. Ninjutsu is the ultimate martial art: a Ninja shows no intention to fight, and perseveres not with some "noble cause" but simply with the spirit of enduring the cruelties of both life and death. His life is a solitary path, bound on either side, as if in a cycle of death and rebirth, by the act of Isshi Sōden (transmission to a sole disciple). His aim is to attain the enlightenment described by the first words of the Buddha: Yuiga Dokuson, "Alone in the world, I am exalted."

NINJA HISTORY

The history of the Ninja is long and ancient. Some say it extends back for over 2,500 years, but in fact there are records going back as far as 4,300 years. It would be fair to say that it has been around ever since homo sapiens first appeared. The original Shinobi no Mono would have developed a wide variety of Shinobi arts using stones,

"Seated immovably in the shadow of glory." The author inside the main hall of Hōkōsha, a shrine on Mt. Togakushi from where his art originated.

sticks, vines and the like. Old stories say that they played an important role as 'behind-the-scenes' forces in Ōkume no Mikoto's nation-building operations and Emperor Jimmu's subjugation of Yamato, which legends place at around 600 BC. Some old documents also state that Price Shōtoku (574–622) used Shinobi.

This venerable Japanese art of Ninjutsu was also subject to influence from overseas. Even today, the Ninpō Taijutsu legacy includes techniques called Senban-nage (throwing of thin iron plates) and Hichō-jutsu (misunderstood by many to mean 'leaping techniques,' although it actually refers to ways of neutralizing the opponent's own techniques). These are part of the Gyokko school of Kosshi-jutsu and the Kotō school of Koppō-jutsu, which were apparently brought to Japan from China by Yao Yu Hu and Zhang Wu Sheng, during the T'ang dynasty (618–907). Another legend says that a T'ang general known as Yi Gou fled to Japan following a military defeat. He landed at Ise, went into hiding, and practiced Zen meditation in the Sada Caves near Iga. Yi Gou was apparently a master of the art of Hichō Ongyō-jutsu, a literally 'super-human' method for hiding from an enemy in order to render their techniques ineffective.

According to the Densho (written records) of the Togakure School, the Togakure style of Ninjutsu was founded by Togakure Daisuke. In 1181, Taira forces set out with tens of thousands of troops in order to subdue Kiso Yoshinaka (1154–84), who had raised an army to overthrow their grip on power. Yoshinaka aimed to intercept them, and commanded his whole army from a cave overlooking the Susobana river, which flows through the Togakure (now called Togakushi) mountains. The place where Yoshinaka stationed his troops and raised the battle cry is known even now as Lord Kiso's Cave. Yoshinaka's forces included a sixteen-year-old vassal named Shima Kosanta Minamoto no Kanesada, who was said to have undergone austere training in the Togakure area and to have mastered Senban-nage and Hichō-jutsu along with similar techniques peculiar to Shugendō, the mountain asceticism which was now spreading throughout the country. Incidentally, Takamatsu Sensei also practiced Shugendō at its most important site, the Kumano mountains, and became its head—the "Top Tengu."

By 1184, Yoshinaka's luck had run out and he died in battle. Kanesada had meanwhile been wounded in many places as he cut his way through 3,000 horsemen under

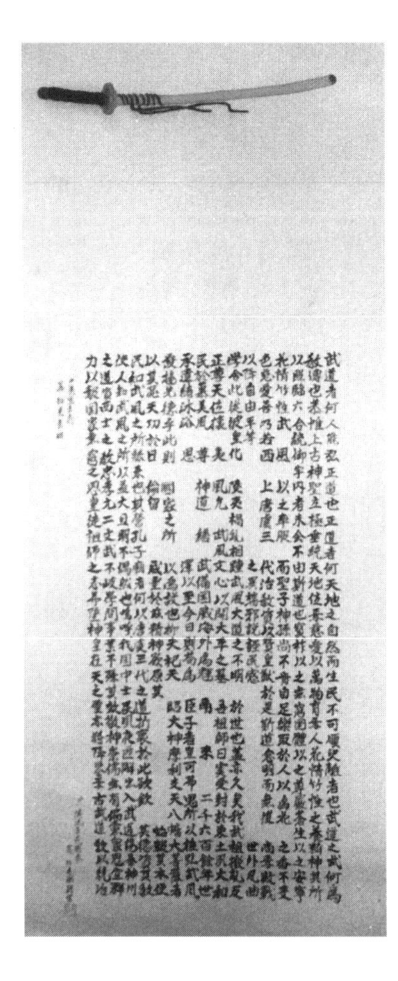

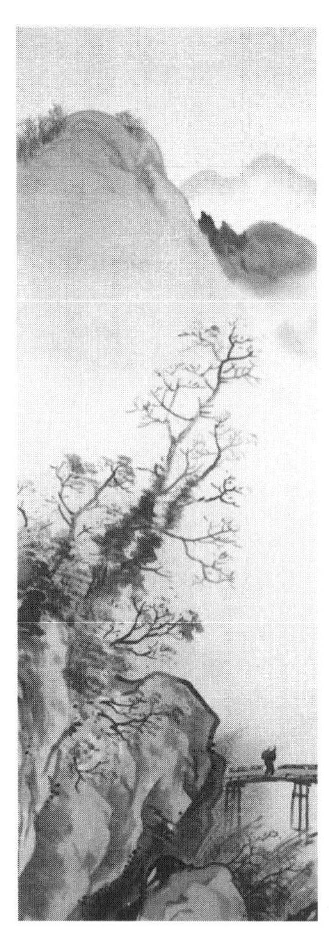

"At last, the days of waiting for happiness are past, and I take up my brush like the Chinese strategist Jiang Taigong"

LEFT: Calligraphy by Takamatsu Sensei: "What are the martial ways?"

RIGHT: The first painting ever given to the author by Takamatsu Sensei

Fujiwara Hidehira, and had collapsed from his severe injuries. He was rescued by a Taoist sage known by the epithet Kasumi-gakure—"Hiding in the mist"—and escaped with him to the mountains of Iga. In time the sage accepted him as his student, and trained him in the martial ways of Ninjutsu. Shima Kosanta Minamoto no Kanesada later changed his name to Togakure Daisuke, and established Togakure-ryū as a new style of Ninjutsu in the Iga area.

It is the way of the world that winners do not cease attacking until they have wiped out their opponents and secured their newly gained position, while the exhausted losers try to escape by heading out into the mountains, far from human habitation. In this way, Fujiwara fugitives, as well as the warriors defeated during the Taira-Minamoto conflict, and later those from the Northern & Southern Courts (1336–92), sought refuge in places such as Iga or Kōga, and established themselves as rural Samurai. However, they were hunted down rigorously, and these rural Samurai found themselves obliged to create and refine Tongyō (evasion) techniques, so that they and their families could escape and survive. It is their research which, systematically enhanced over time, gave birth to Ninjutsu, Ninpō Taijutsu.

On the other hand, the proximity of these rural Samurai to Kyōto meant that they were ideally placed to be 'early adopters' of the newly imported science of explosives, which they combined with home-grown Ninja tools. They were also exposed to foreign philosophies such as Qimen Dunjia (directional divination related to Feng Shui), which entered Japan via the "three roads"—the two overland Silk Roads and the marine Silk Road. If the occasion arose, they would enter the field and exert themselves on the side of justice, for example by gathering troops loyal to the Imperial Court.

NINJUTSU DIVERSITY

I have learned many schools of Ninjutsu via Isshi Sōden—Togakure-ryū, Kotō-ryū, Gyokko-ryū, Kumogakure-ryū, Gyokushin-ryū, Gikan-ryū, and so on—and now discharge my duties as their grandmaster. There were, however, many more schools in the past: according to one theory, as many as seventy-three. Some of the principal ones were Negishi-ryū, Shirai-ryū, Shintō-ryū, Hakuun-ryū, Kōshū-ryū, Kishū-ryū, Gen-ryū, Gen-jitsu-ryū, Ryūmon-ryū, Tentonhappō-ryū, Gotonjuppō-ryū, Kurama-ryū, Yasuda-ryū, Iga-ryū, and Kōga-ryū. Iga-ryū and Kōga-ryū were particularly well known.

Scholars put forth all sorts of theories—that there were seventy-plus schools, seventy-five schools, 103 schools, and so on. Nobody really knows the true number. In any case, if one did know the truth about Ninjutsu, it would no longer be true Ninjutsu. Samurai soap operas on Japanese television often feature the "Shadow Yagyū" warriors, despite the fact that there is apparently no basis for them in historical records. Nevertheless, the Yagyū Shinkage sword school founded by Yagyū Sekishūsai Muneyoshi (1529–1606) was situated in Iga, so it would seem foolish to deny the possibility entirely.

The Muromachi (1392–1568) and Edo (1600–1868) periods saw the rise and fall of numerous feudal domains. It is generally believed that each domain would have had at least a few Ninja. Even if there were no Ninja per se, spying and strategy would have been carried out under the command of Bushi or the like (in the Edo period, Bushi had the highest status in the warrior-farmer-artisan-merchant social hierarchy). There would also have been special, unconventional organizations whose existence must not be overlooked. The nature of these Ninja or Bushi would change depending on the period, circumstances, and attitudes. It is easy to picture these Ninja blending into their surroundings, surviving as well as they could within the constraints of the Shinobi no Mono lifestyle.

NINJA KNOWLEDGE ENCOMPASSED ALL MARTIAL WAYS

My teacher once described Ninjutsu to me as follows: "It is said that Ninja knew all the martial ways. In each, they would undergo at least the minimum training essential to their life as a Ninja. They would study the eight branches of Ninja Hachimon: Ninja Kiai (energy harmonization), Koppō Taijutsu, Ninpō swordwork, spearwork, Shuriken, fire, traditional arts, and general knowledge."

In other words, life as a Shinobi started with the Ninja Hachimon. Over time, however, this changed so that greater weight was placed on Happō Hiken. The Shinobi Happō Hiken consist of the following:

1) Taijutsu, Hichō-jutsu, Nawa-nage (body skills and rope-throwing)
2) Karate Koppō Taijutsu, Jūtaijutsu (unarmed fighting)
3) Sō-jutsu, Naginata-jutsu (spear and halberd arts)
4) Bō-jutsu, Jō-jutsu, Hanbō-jutsu (staff and stick arts)
5) Senban-nage, Ken-nage-jutsu, Shuriken (throwing of blades)
6) Ka-jutsu, Sui-jutsu (use of fire and water)
7) Chikujō Gunryaku Hyōhō (military fortification, strategy and tactics)
8) Onshin-jutsu (concealment)

The branches listed above were known as the Happō (eight methods), and were supplemented by Hiken-jutsu (secret sword arts), in other words, the Shinobi sword, Kodachi (short sword), Jutte (truncheon) and Tessen (metal fan), to complete the Ninja Happō Hiken.

In later periods the term Togakure-ryū Jūhakkei (eighteen forms) was also used. The eighteen forms of the Shinobi were defined as "Spiritual education, Koppō-jutsu body skills, swordwork, stickwork, Shuriken, Kusari-gama (sickle & chain), spear, halberd, horsemanship, water training, explosives, strategy, espionage, infiltration, concealment, disguise, and climatic & environmental knowledge." These were obliterated by—or rather concealed within—the Bugei Jūhappan (eighteen types of conventional martial art), thereby escaping through transformation into thirty-six forms: discretion became the better part of valor. In a sense, they evolved into the thirty-six Togakure strategies, the Kuji of the Santō Tonkō techniques, and even the Jūji principle of bonding with the divine.

In fact, Ninja did not simply learn all forms of martial arts through their training: they continued studying until they reached a level far beyond mere technical prowess.

NINPŌ TRAINING

The first step in Ninpō training is that of physical endurance. The important thing here is to polish your techniques, use your spirit, and endure physical forces until you reach a critical state where everything is on the line.

The second step is that of mental and emotional endurance. If an animal encounters an enemy, it generally bares its teeth straight away and launches into a fight. However, no matter how fearsome the enemy, human beings have the ability to laugh. Even if somebody comes to cut at you with a sword, as long as your heart does not waver you can smile at them, endure the situation physically and flee without injuring them. My teacher used to say, "Harmony has supreme importance in a warrior's heart." This concept of "harmony" really refers to the fact that everything in the universe is connected,

The "Takamagahara Amatsu Tatara Hibun" referred to by the famous poet Ōtomo no Yakamochi means "To know the way of spiritual and martial study through the power of nature."

Ōkume no Mikoto is said to have been the first Shinobi. In the "era of the gods," Shinobi were compared to three-legged crows. (Picture by the author)

Sakanoue no Tamuramaro, a general who was also an ancestor of the Ninja

everything in nature, all the seasons, love and hate, good and evil—all are interconnected aspects of a fundamental unity.

The third step is the endurance of knowledge. The word "knowledge" (Shiki) can also be interpreted phonetically as "four fears." The image here is that someone at the top of a pyramid (in the metaphorical sense too) can see clearly in all four directions, gaining in the same way a comprehensive, balanced understanding of nature's cycles (i.e. the four seasons), and that this perspective frees you from fear. While mental and emotional endurance can be an active process of setting your mind to endure, enduring knowledge goes beyond both physical and emotional endurance to a level where you develop the power to understand everything without conscious thought. This means not just responding to things that have already happened, but sensing things that are about to happen and handling them naturally. In other words, enduring knowledge is connected with having a rich education, while also practicing endurance with respect to one's own sixth sense and subconscious mind.

Learning Hanbōjutsu (Three-foot stick techniques)

ESSENCE OF A NINJA

Ninja aspired to merge their spirit and techniques into one, and become 'uncommon' common people. Some people did try to become 'superhuman' through their training in Ninpō, but they did not achieve great success as Ninja. It is quite easy to become a superman; Ninjutsu makes one more aware of just how difficult it is to become a 'normal' human being.

The essence of being a Shinobi was to focus strongly on natural providence, on what the heavens and earth provided. This gave birth to Sakki-jutsu or Sacchi-hō, methods for anticipating and sensing. Ninja knew the laws of Nature, and were thus able to sense great changes in the natural world. They would make skillful use of natural conditions or disasters to apply Ninjutsu just when appropriate. This is what is meant by Tenmon, one branch of their martial studies.

For example, if they noticed sparrows or chickens scratching for food late in the evening or searching for a sleeping place high up in some dense woodland, or large numbers of fireflies or other insects flying indoors in summer, or carp splashing around on the surface of some water, they would understand these as being precursors to rain. Conversely, if kites flew circles high in the sky and sparrows and chickens went to roost early, barely bothering to forage for food, this was taken to herald fine weather. If insects that normally lived at the tops of trees moved down, if the normally high-flying

The author asking Takamatsu Sensei a question

larks gave their distinctive call from lower reaches, and if the leaves of reeds, pampas grass, or common grass lay on their side, they predicted a storm coming.

Ninja always paid great attention to daily matters like these. If they detected a stimulus from the outside world, no matter how slight, they would respond immediately. This is because they made sure to maintain their surroundings in such a state that they could react instantaneously to any change, never being surprised. Someone with a sense for survival: that was the essence of a Ninja.

NINJA'S ORAL TRADITIONS

Ninja had many oral traditions (Kuden). Almost all of Ninpō were passed down in this way, man to man. Kuden can also be interpreted phonetically as "nine transmissions." In antiquity nine was seen as the highest number, and believed to transmit the essence of divinity. These man-to-man Kuden were used to transmit the doctrine of the mystic nine-syllable Kuji. A master would select a sole student to receive the teaching, and pass on the law that divine warriors do not kill.

Kaga no Chiyo (1703–75) wrote a Haiku which goes as follows:

Asagao ni	A morning glory
Tsurube torarete	Has usurped my well bucket
Morai mizu	I can go next door

Another well-known poem, by Matsuo Bashō (1644–94), says:

Shizukasa-ya	Summer quietness
Iwa ni shimi-iru	Cicada voices burrow
Semi no koe	Into the cliffside

In Haiku, individual poems like these are each referred to as a "Ku," but the character "Ku" originally refers to a huge number somewhat like the Hindi "shankh" (a hundred thousand trillion), expressing an immense conception of the universe. Just like these Haiku conjuring up infinite aromas, each short phrase in a Shinobi Kuden encom-

The author's treasure: fifteen years' worth of letters from Takamatsu Sensei

"Once a year I talk with my teacher, when I show my students the Densho"

passes incredibly broad, deep, and diverse meanings. Incidentally, Japan's Kamiyomoji (an indigenous Japanese script which existed before Chinese characters were imported—allegedly 'since the age of the gods') also includes words which convey the whole of creation in just a few characters. This was also a Kuden.

Many martial artists gained great renown by serving the people in power at the time. However, it would be a serious mistake to assume that these 'Bugeisha,' were wonderful people or had true ability just because their names have been passed down over the generations. In every period of history there would be fighters—some serving the government or a lord, some not—who earnestly refined their heart, body, and techniques in the Ninja way. They would not appear in the history books, but remain aloof from the world, always out in the field as ordinary people, with only the earth and the sky for companions, unaffected by the changes and currents of their time.

Takamatsu Sensei's own teacher, Toda Shinryūken—the 32nd Grandmaster of Togakure-ryū Ninpō—taught Budō as chief instructor at a martial academy in Kyōto, and enjoyed an excellent reputation. He was asked to do this by Matsudaira Noriyasu (1794–1870), one of the Shogunate's senior councillors. However, political changes meant that Matsudaira Noriyasu lost his position, and Toda Shinryūken immediately left the academy, traveling around the Kinki area, keeping his whereabouts hidden. He never again took up an official post.

Ninjutsu has always been passed down by Ninja who managed to find their way through the midst of confusion and destruction and to survive, whether in the Sengoku period (1482–1558), the turbulent times at the Edo/Meiji transition (1868), or the First and Second World Wars. Takamatsu Sensei himself went to China, survived encounters with notorious martial artists and other enemies with designs on his life, and became feared as "The Mongolian Tiger." Having waded through carnage, he returned to Japan in 1919, and commented on this episode as follows: "My training in Japan, followed by my experience of ten years of actual combat in China, enabled me to understand the essence of the martial arts and the importance of Ninjutsu." Sensei was a genuine professor of the otherworldly science of Budō Ninpō.

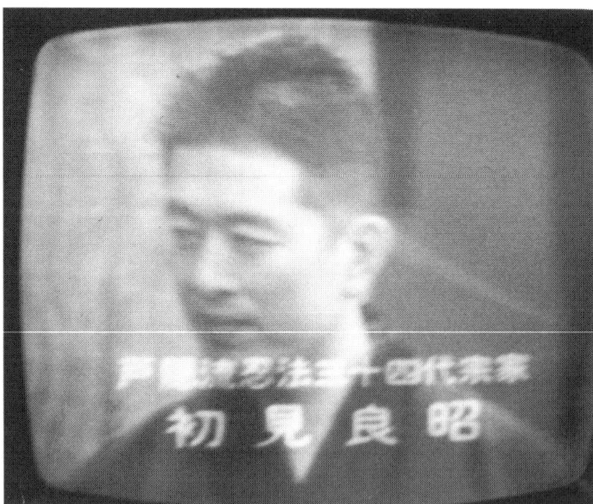

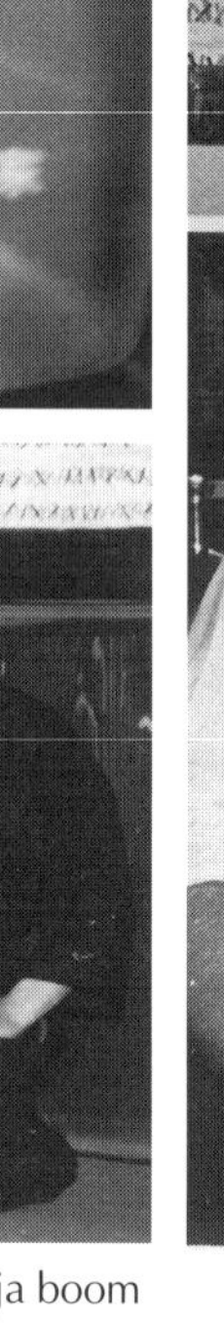

The author at the time of the first post-war Ninja boom

GOTON NO JUTSU

Examine the character "Ton" as used above in Tongyō ("hiding one's form"; or alternatively, "the discretion doctrine"), and you can discover it to be a combination of the characters 'fleeing' with a 'shield'—just as along the path of Ninpō. The principle of recognizing the value gained by winning through flight is one of Ninjutsu's cardinal rules. However, it is not simply a question of escaping. What can one use as a shield? One can use the Five Elements (wood, fire, earth, metal, and water), the Five Rings, the Five Ways (the way of enlightenment), the Five Arts, the Five Teachings, the Five Confucian Virtues (benevolence, righteousness, propriety, wisdom, and sincerity), Nature, the shining (or shadowed) glory of the martial ways, beliefs, politics (or rather, policies for life)—the shields are multiple and varied.

As you can see, the number five and its associated sound "Go" are important as indicators of comprehensiveness and completion. In Ninjutsu, Goton no Jutsu refers to five arts—Mokuton, Katon, Doton, Kinton, and Suiton—meaning evasion through the means of wood, fire, earth, metal, and water, respectively. For example, hiding underground or digging a trap-hole would be Doton no Jutsu, while using fire or explosives to dazzle an opponent and flee would be Katon. Goton no Jutsu is alive even now, even though the particular tools employed may have changed. People engaged in war make great use of 'uninhabitable' places, such as forests or deserts—these are their modern castles. Sounds, colors, smells. . . Ninja utilize all six senses—maybe even more—to detect danger, distract their opponents, and escape via Tongyō.

BUDŌ IS ONLY FOR THOSE WHOSE HEART IS IN THE RIGHT PLACE

Ninjutsu was not actually "Ninjutsu" right from the start. It started out as "Shinobi methods" (Shinobi no Hō), meaning methods for discerning what is right for the world, enduring, training to become a moral being, becoming aware of one's destiny, and dedicating one's life to other people or the world as a whole. These later became known as Ninpō, and later still Ninjutsu. The original sense was not one of mere Jutsu (techniques), but rather that of Hō (laws or principles) permeating the entire universe. For this reason, Ninja always fixed their perspective on Tenchijin, the relationship between the universe, the earth, and humankind.

In *Ninjutsu Hiketsubun*, a Kuden by Takamatsu Sensei, he talks quite clearly about the essence of Shinobi: "The essence of the martial arts and the ways of strategy lies in protecting oneself. Ninjutsu is central to this self-protection. Ninjutsu protects the spirit too. If you perform the martial arts with an incorrect spirit, instead of protecting yourself, you will end up killing yourself."

The same is true, for example, for medicine: it is designed to save people, but if applied the wrong way it can kill them. Similarly, we consume our daily food and drink to maintain and protect our health, but those who consume too much end up harming their own bodies. Ministers have a duty to govern their country, and their prime responsibility is surely to protect the lives of their people; yet they may lack insight or suffer from self-interest, with the result that their own lives assume the greatest importance, they deteriorate into wicked individuals tormenting their people, and the country consequently goes to ruin.

The same applies to the martial arts. If a martial arts adept studies the essence of Shinobi, which is so vital for protecting oneself, and learns its skills, they will also gain the secret of Kanjin Kaname: "what is truly important." So what *is* truly important? Kanjin Kaname can also be written as "the heart and eyes of the gods," and thus it means the way of heaven, or the laws of heaven. Put another way: the truth of heaven, or (to clarify this for those with fixed notions of what 'heaven' entails) the principles of nature. There is no evil in the way of heaven, the laws of heaven, the truth of heaven, the principles of nature. There is just faith in the great laws. For example, take the five elements—wood, fire, metal, water. . . and earth. Without earth, none of the others could exist. Having no earth in the five elements would be like having no truth in heaven.

If a person acts truthfully, in a just manner, they will be in accord with this way of heaven. If they are in accord with the way of heaven, the will of heaven will be done. This is the heart and the eyes of the gods, Kanjin Kaname—the vital essence of Shinobi.

The most important thing in Ninjutsu is to have a warrior's heart. Takamatsu Sensei always used to say, "The heart of a warrior means a sincere heart. As Kajō Chikusei teaches us, one must strive to be as gentle as a flower, and as straight—moreover, as straightforward—as bamboo." The essence of a flower is nature at work, the essence of bamboo is a natural way of life. Ninjutsu is a great warrior's path open only to those whose heart is in the right place.

KYOJITSU: MANIPULATING PERCEPTIONS OF TRUTH

There is a poem from martial arts' history which reads: "People think they perform their techniques themselves. . . unaware that their bodies are guided by the gods." Those intent on 'putting on' techniques or becoming more skillful are sure to fail in the long run. It is more important to move in step with the gods, maintain a disinterested attitude, keep control over one's own emotions, and retain a sensibility which goes beyond the everyday.

Ninjutsu is the art of escaping, and there are innumerable ways of doing this. Indeed, if you analyze the Japanese character for "escape," you can find linguistic links with other characters meaning "going beyond" and "one trillion." The myriad forms of Ninjutsu, an art of evasion as well as escape, are sometimes described as having "1,000 forms, 10,000 variations," but these links show that it ought really to be expressed as "1,000 forms, infinite variations." At the same time, it is important to realize that there is no need to concentrate on fine details (another character linked to those above). Just as in Zen, it is by stripping off the superfluous and abstracting until only the essence is left that one comes to understand the true nature of Ninpō Taijutsu. It is certainly not something which ought to be explained in minute detail through the medium of words.

The Ninja view of the universe contains not only three dimensions but four. The fourth dimension is that of the world of Mu—nothingness—a world haunted by death, a world of spirit only. It is a world with no physical existence, where everything simply disappears. That is why in that world you must not let an opponent see or sense your form—you must wipe it out entirely.

The vast majority of Ninjutsu practitioners are, however, stuck at the third dimension, or even the second. Some people are in fact still in the first dimension—maybe even some 'minus' level! It is only once you can move as freely as a phantom from the first dimension to the fourth (each dimension has positive and negative versions too), and discover how all things arise from the nothingness of the "Mu" dimension, that you can become a true Ninja, one of the Four Heavenly Ninja Kings. This will lead you to discover the fundamental, final step leading through to the fifth dimension.

What I would most like you, the readers, to learn from this book is that the key to the martial arts, to Ninpō Taijutsu, is not power. I would like you to look at the aesthetics of space—rainbows, auroras, and so on—find a way through to the world of Mu, and then, standing in the realm of Kū, the Void, discover for yourselves some hint as to how truth

1

2

3

4

5

6

7

Using films, television, plays, and lectures to spread the word about Ninjutsu. 1: presenting a talk on Ninjutsu to Crown Prince Akihito (the current Emperor) at Gakushūin University. 2: with TV presenter Honma Chiyoko. 3: with TV presenter Takahashi Keizō and actor Ichikawa Raizō. 4: with actors Ichikawa Utaemon and Kitaōji Kin'ya. 5: with actor Chiba Shin'ichi ("Sonny Chiba"). 6: the author with his co-stars in the TV series "Ninja Olympiad" (a.k.a. "Jiraiya"). 7: with actors Maki Fuyukichi and Ōse Kōichi.

and falsehood can be freely manipulated in the fourth dimension. Five was regarded as the highest number in ancient times because it symbolized going beyond this fourth dimension. For example, five would be used to refer to the Son of Heaven (the Emperor) or a Lord, while four would signify the four heavenly kings supporting him.

Dr. Nitobe Inazō (1862–1933) swore when he was a student that his wish was "to become a bridge over the Pacific," and true to his words, he later became Under Secretary-General of the League of Nations. He is best known, however, for his book *Bushido,* first published in 1899. This book is often noted as "the best way to learn about Japan's spiritual background." The author himself, though, often stressed that "it is important to read between the lines." The same applies to Makimono or Densho, written transmissions of the martial arts that are handed down from a master to those students who attain Menkyo Kaiden (the level where all basic licenses have been awarded, and a student is ready to begin studying the finer points of the art). Only people of great wisdom and immense skill have the ability to seek out the hidden truths which lie concealed between the lines of text in these documents.

Incidentally, the book *Bushido* was written, published, and widely read at a time when Japan had suddenly attracted the attention of the world by winning the Sino-Japanese War (1894–95) and Russo-Japanese War (1905–06). There is always a historical background to historic publications of this kind.

The space between the lines has the power to give readers "vocational insight." In this book, I present many valuable techniques and concepts, hitherto unpublished, with the balanced aid of text and photographs; but I hope that you read between the lines to capture the inexpressible principles and truths of the martial arts. I am sure they will serve as guiding principles for your life. Of course, even if you are unable to read between the lines, that does not matter. I am sure you will still be able to grasp something of value from this book.

The monk Tōsui, who abandoned his Dōjō, became a priest and attained enlightenment. (Picture by the author.)

The ceremony of transmitting a license is at the same time a way of leaving transmitted knowledge behind.

A poem by Reitetsu expressing the essence of the art: "People believe that they perform techniques with their own strength, unaware that it is actually the gods who guide their actions." Reitetsu was one of Takamatsu Sensei's noms de plume. Picture by the author; title: Bunraku ("the joy of listening"; also puppet theater)

Ninniku Seishin: the spirit of forbearance

Chapter 2

Ninpō Taijutsu

忍法体術

NINPŌ TAIJUTSU

The Ninpō tradition includes the Ninja's unique Taijutsu (body arts) and fighting arts, also known as Ninpō Taijutsu, Koppō-jutsu or Kosshi-jutsu. These arts were designed for life, and for survival. Taijutsu was also essential for Ninja to perform their remarkable techniques, using assorted Ninja tools and equipment. These body arts are strong and pliant; they can respond to any kind of change, and can be applied to any situation. One feature of Ninpō Taijutsu is that "Sente" is not allowed: in other words, you never strike the first blow. Also, Ninja who had trained fully in Taijutsu would only need to shed another person's blood in exceptional circumstances.

In the martial arts, the basics are of supreme importance. In general, students start by learning forms or techniques. Beginners have to train initially with "visible" movements: this is inescapable, as otherwise they simply will not understand any further complexities. Visible movements are studied first in Ninpō Taijutsu too—but soon you have to progress to a world which is invisible to the naked eye. It is important that this training be natural. It may be a truism to say that all things in nature are natural, but most people live and are "educated" in the narrow world of human beings, and end up thinking of things in an excessively complicated way, thereby losing their ability to see things straight and naturally.

Ninpō Taijutsu did in fact vary greatly depending on the period, and from area to area. In each variant, however, there were both basic forms and progressive forms. There were also key points found in the forms of all of the different schools, while each form would itself exhibit infinite variations, from motionless Kamae onwards. These variations should be treasured. I really want people to understand this feeling. A single form may end up appearing totally different as a result of these variations.

Some people see the techniques I perform and call them Kamiwaza, divine techniques. They call me a divine warrior. Yet if these techniques were something I had produced myself, there would be nothing special about them at all. I never perform "my" techniques. Even at my age, I am still merely carrying out techniques as I was taught them by Takamatsu Sensei. Otherwise, techniques that have been polished and handed down over generations, for hundreds and thousands of years, would actually deteriorate. As techniques are transmitted, life itself is received.

Hand training: Taijutsu trained through energy and endurance.
Ninja train their hands, fingers, and fists.

"Nin" (calligraphy by the author)

My intention is always to live by some words I heard from my teacher Takamatsu Sensei: "However much I study, it is never enough." He himself continued refining his techniques throughout his life. This "life of study" feels like, indeed sounds like, a message that is constantly being broadcast to me in my master's voice. It tells me that the important thing in life is to keep pursuing the truths which lie behind everything.

THE NEVER-ENDING MARTIAL WAY

The martial ways have always been a part of the Ninjutsu tradition. I once did some calligraphy, writing "I am a lion." Fine words, perhaps, but the true meaning only becomes apparent when you add the small letter の between two of the characters: then it reads "I am no more than a child of my teacher."

Ninjutsu is the essence of life, the truth of life, the wisdom of life, the feeling required for life, and an art of a thousand forms, innumerable variations. Compare this with religion: if religion becomes fixed, static, and stays confined within its own modes of thought, the result—regrettably—is religious war, or recurrent violence from those who claim to be serving God. The original essence of religion is to aim at achieving harmony and balance with the natural world. Yet in the current age it seems that this type of self-awareness, a living concept that in Ninjutsu at least is transmitted from a master to his students and then helped to grow, is somewhat lacking in almost every one of the world's religions. Take for example the words reputed to have been said by the Buddha: "Alone in the world, I am exalted." These words contain Kyojitsu—both truth and falsehood.

There is a didactic poem which, somewhat paraphrased, reads as follows: "Alpha's children create and nurture Omega before returning home to Alpha." These are words of life, full of knowledge, which explain the cycle of life and rebirth. One interpretation of this poem is that first Shintō was born and people learned it, then Buddhism was introduced, then they returned to Shintō. It therefore signifies that we live within a large cycle of rebirth and development or growth. For example, grass you believed to have withered in winter sprouts again the following spring. It makes you think it is dead, while in reality it is not. Life in nature follows cycles and grows, but humans seem incapable of perceiving this in any other way than the simplistic view that things are "either dead or alive."

This poem also reveals the transmission of life, spirit, and technique, which links a master to his pupils—referred to in Ninjutsu as Isshi Sōden—and whereby the master's pupils eventually grow into masters themselves and raise their own pupils. This transmission depends on something that is often referred to in the arts as Alpha-Omega breathing. It is akin to the relationship between close friends who understand each other without the need for words. There is a proverb which says, "The relationship between parent and child lasts for a lifetime, that between husband and wife for this life and the next, but that between master and disciple endures for three lifetimes, the

In Taijutsu, one must walk the path of natural power. Shiraha-dori Kikaku-gata (top) and Katon Taijutsu-gata (bottom)

past, present, and future." This 'three lifetimes' principle truly reflects the essence of the martial arts and Ninjutsu.

Kosshi-jutsu is another name for Ninpō Taijutsu. The word "Kosshi" refers to the core of an art, the most important part. That is why Kosshi-jutsu became the Taijutsu of Ninpō. The similar term Koppō-jutsu originated from arts such as the tea ceremony or Koto (zither) playing, where "Koppō" is used to refer to the knack or some finer points of skill.

The ultimate secret of the martial arts is certainly not to be found in forms or Kata (formal sets of movements). Those who focus on forms or Kata get trapped by them, and become unable to perform free, living movements. In a field of combat they might well end up dead. The real 'secret' lies inside your heart. That is why people who aspire to the martial arts must have a true heart, as I mentioned before. Moreover, they must maintain it constantly. The most important thing is to have compassion at every step along the martial way, and to hold a sense of due respect toward the arts themselves.

THE SECRET OF WINNING

One never knows when a fight might start. That is why in Budō one keeps prepared, so that should a fight arise, one can settle it as quickly as possible. In a dangerous situation, you act swiftly, without any hesitation. That is the secret of winning. If you have to fight, remember that you have been entrusted with a mission and are serving a greater purpose; you must *KNOW* that you can win, and use this energy in your encounter.

In Shintō there is a word, "Nakaima," which literally means "the middle of now." It teaches us that the current moment embodies the whole of time, and consequently, that how you live the current moment is of supreme importance. In the martial arts too, including Ninjutsu, each individual moment is important. It is vital to live through each moment to the full, without wasting time on pointless political maneuvering.

One adjective that has often been used to describe Ninja is "bug-like." At first this might seem like an insult, but in fact it is not. As it happens, the Japanese word for "bug" sounds just the same as other words signifying "free from ego" or "without intention." My teacher also told me the following: "If it holds onto a horse's tail, even a lowly bug can travel a thousand, or even a trillion miles." Furthermore, it is important to remember that dragons and reptiles are also "bugs." Another common phrase in Japanese is "the bugs told me," meaning to have a premonition; and these people described as "bug-like" did indeed pass on information. In other words, a true interpretation of this phrase demonstrates how Ninja acted as an essential medium, important personnel sending vital transmissions and receiving indispensable messages.

Reptile worship is quite common in all areas of the globe—and Ninja were very skillful at using such creatures. Ninja would change their form in the same way that certain

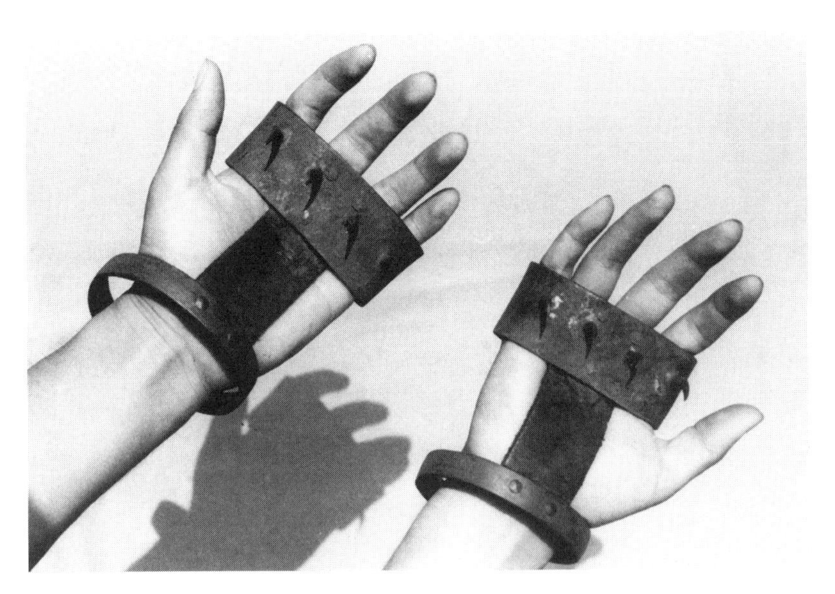

Shukō (above) and Sokkō (right): the hand and foot claws used in Ninpō Taijutsu

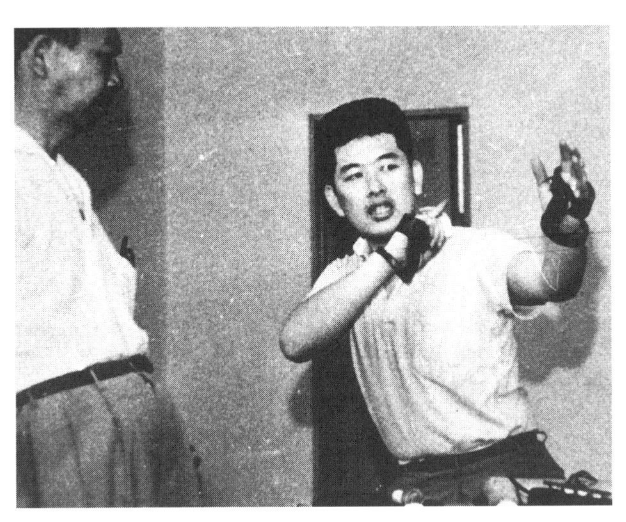

The author in his role as martial arts consultant to Yamamoto Satsuo, director of the film *Shinobi no Mono*

Ryūton no Jutsu—dragon-style evasion

reptiles do, somewhat like the Kabuki plays where an actor rapidly performs seven shape-shifts. And while they were able to enter into the forms of the martial arts, they could also escape outside the forms. Dragons, one form of mythical reptile, grow by shedding their skin; chameleons are the same. Likewise, beetles such as the cicada gain the ability to fly by shedding their skin. Ninja would have watched the reptiles and studied how they were at one with nature, transforming themselves and living freely. The next time you spot a snake or a lizard, try copying its movements. Ninjutsu also contains related techniques for disguise, called Shichihō Sanpō-gata (the seven ways and three methods).

One more feature of snakes and other reptiles that should not be overlooked is hibernation. During this time, they slow their breathing and survive the harshness of winter. If a Ninja realized that the right opportunity had not yet presented itself, he would sit quietly and wait for spring. He would bide his time, await an opportunity, measure the moment, and, once he realized that his chance had arrived, suddenly emerge to attack.

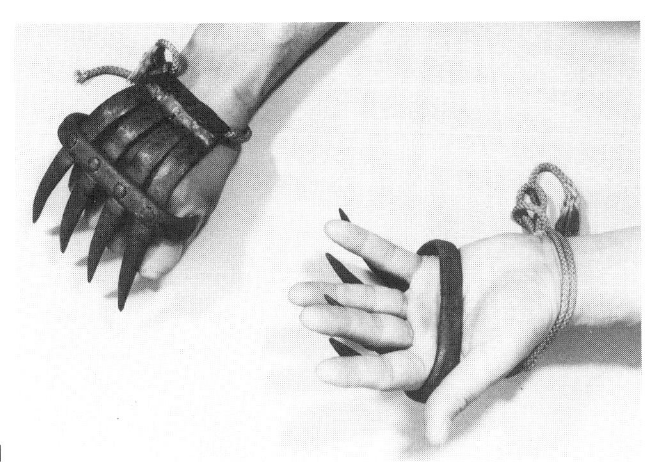

Shukō from a different school

One principle of the martial arts is to have a heart or spirit which is flexible enough to cope with anything. Above all, the basis of Budō is Juppō Sesshō no Jutsu ('contact in ten directions'), which is also known as Jūtai-jutsu. For example, audiences are often stunned by techniques such as "Ninja Mutō-dori," where an unarmed Ninja disarms a sword-wielding opponent; these techniques were borne from Juppō Sesshō no Jutsu. Juppō Sesshō describes a situation when two heroic creatures—a dragon and a tiger—fight using a vast array of techniques (see p.176). One can interpret this as indicating that Budō and Ninjutsu exist both inside and outside the box; indeed at a level totally beyond everything else. People are free to make or break such boxes. If one can enter in, one can also take things out—which is what Budō and Ninpō Taijutsu are all about.

In Ninpō Taijutsu, we train in unique Ninpō techniques called Kihon Happō: the "basic eight." These Kihon Happō are the starting point for Taijutsu, and at the same time, something to which you return after acquiring other Ninja moves. They are basic techniques, but at the same time more important than anything else. Certain numbers offer secret teachings in Budō and Ninpō Taijutsu, and eight is one of them. If you place the figure 8 on its side, you get "∞": infinity. In other words, this is an alphabetical, alpha-omega continuity which also signifies a chain—the chain of life. As you can see from this, 8 actually means both the beginning and the end: it is infinite. Any technique has α and β aspects. Similarly, the 'basic' techniques of Kihon Happō are in fact without limit. It is also enlightening to consider the Daruma principle: even if you fall seven times, rise eight times and you are ahead.

The techniques of Ninpō Taijutsu incorporate changes—in other words, Kyojitsu Tenkan-hō, the interchange of truth and falsehood. For example, if an enemy suddenly attacks and you are grappling hard, you might indicate that you are going to pull with the right hand, leap in on the left and then throw, but in fact you enter in on the right and throw them on that side. Show a feint, execute a real move; show a real move as a feint then do it for real; show a real move but make them think it is a feint, then do a real feint—the interchange between false and real develops freely through the technique. That is how the value, the victory, and the vitality of the technique arise.

Togakure-ryū Ninpō Taijutsu also contains sharp, fast combat moves where an otherwise unarmed Ninja would fight using his tools.

KAMAE AND THEIR FORMS

This may sound strange, but those who train in the martial arts for many years ought to develop a physique, stance, and behavior that do not immediately reveal them to be a martial artist. In most cases, however, you can tell immediately what art they have studied. This is extremely dangerous in the world of real combat, because their weak areas can be easily attacked. For this reason, I always warn my students not to show the demeanor of a martial artist, and they live such ordinary lives that those around say about them, "Such a high grade? I'd never have thought it!" This is the "normal form," one of the stances in the Shinobi Shichihō Sanpō-gata. Of course, they are not simply living oblivious to their surroundings. They are cultivating "Heijōshin" (equanimity), so that they can respond to and assess even the smallest stimulus from the outside world.

In Ninpō and the ways of martial strategy, the three types of Kamae have much in common: Tai-gamae (body stances), Jin-gamae (battle formations), and Shiro-gamae (castle positions). The determination hidden inside each of these Kamae reveals itself as the power of one's spirit. For example, there is a document in the Gyokko school called Shinpi Kohyō Hibun ('Secret Book of the Tiger & Cub Mysteries'), which includes a stance called Komochi-tora no Kamae ('Kamae of tiger with cub'). For this stance, you clasp your hands together in Kongō Gasshō to symbolize unification with everything else in the universe, and concentrate simply on "Perseverance" and a wish to avoid conflict. However, this is backed up by the life-or-death readiness of a tiger protecting its cub. A parent tiger will not fight until the very last moment. In this Kamae your eyes burn bright, as you hope for peace and pray that the enemy does not attack.

THROWS

Throws in Ninpō Taijutsu show immense variety. Once you have learned the individual Taijutsu throwing techniques, you move on to combining these throws. This means understanding their flow and practicing it, and also forms part of Randori (free practice). Another feature which differentiates Ninpō Taijutsu throws from those commonly seen in Jūdō and Aikidō is that you let the opponent throw you. Then, just at the moment when they relax, thinking they have won, you knock them down by applying a lock or strike. There are countless techniques like this.

Jūdō practitioners often declare what their favorite techniques are; their Tokui-waza. That is fine in the world of sport, as it is simply a matter of winning, losing, or drawing. If a strategist living in a world at war were to announce his favorite technique, however, that technique would soon be manipulated and transformed into one leading him on to his own death. The professionals do not readily talk about their favorite moves.

Once my students have been training for some years, I teach them that if they consider Tokui-waza a strength, they should rather not think about their strengths. Otherwise their favorite techniques would become a target for research by their enemies, and

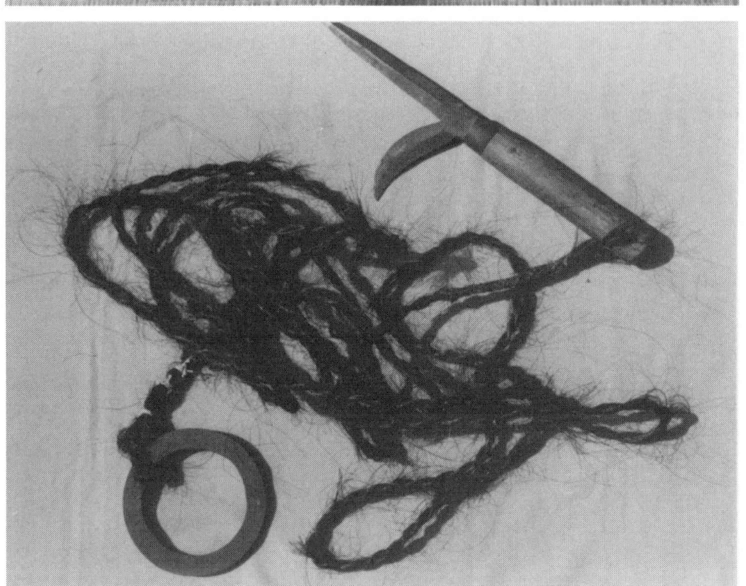

Kyogetsu Shōge. A piece of equipment for entwining, enwrapping, and controlling opponents. It is also said to be a precursor of the Kusarigama. Kyogetsu means" to roam over the hills and dales," while Shōge refers to the hair of women or wild beasts.

actually become a weakness. The future lies rather in knowing your own weaknesses. Opponents will always aim for your weak spots. If you can eliminate all weak spots, you will evidently have only strengths—and provided you persist in the martial ways, you will cease to be proud of these strengths. Any wasted effort will disappear from your movements quite naturally, and your strengths will become as zero. It is essential to recognize the importance of this 'zero feeling.' Tokui-waza should really be interpreted as divine techniques, only available to those destined to learn them through consistent training in the arts.

One phrase I particularly like was written by Toda Shinzaburō Masahide of the Togakure-ryū, and goes as follows: "One should be neither strong nor weak, neither soft nor hard. Leave such thoughts behind, awaken to the Void, and make your body Null to abide by this." This means that in Budō, it is naïve to get caught up in thoughts of strong weak or soft/hard; in the end, even concepts such as skillful/unskillful simply fade away. Jūtaijutsu contains fifteen strong arts and fifteen weak arts, making thirty in total, which can be seen as three sets of ten (as in Sanshin no Kata: Tenchijin and the

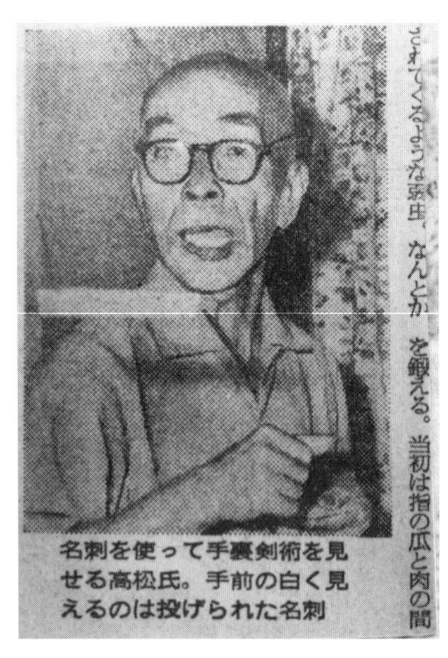

A newspaper article describing Takamatsu Sensei as a Shuriken expert

Jūji idea). Nevertheless, one deliberately and willfully eliminates all of that to make oneself Void.

This in turn allows the desire for a quest to disappear so that one can return to a more natural form. Let us imagine for the moment that you were proud of your skill as an expert technician. You should discard the 'bad habit' of being skillful and instead endeavor to become unskillful! Truly arcane techniques are borne out of this world of the Void.

Still, some people in the martial arts are driven by a desire to "become strong," "get rich," or "gain power." They rush headlong onto a path of wickedness, before meeting with disaster. Being able to live as an ordinary human being is a luxury, it is the most virtuous accomplishment one can have, yet I wonder how many people truly understand this?

THE PATH TO KOBUDŌ

When I was very young I practiced Kendō, also training in Jūdō from my third year at primary school and Karate from my fourth year. In year six I started entering gymnastics competitions. This might lead some people to jump to the conclusion that I have been exceptionally coordinated ever since I was a small boy, but this is certainly not the case—perhaps I was merely trying to make up for the fact that I broke my leg when in year two. When I started Jūdō I was a weak child, and always lost in practice sessions. My mother was convinced that white rice, white sugar, and boiled water (rather than fresh water) were best, and this diet had left me prone to sickness.

However, once I broadened my diet, I rapidly gained strength. In year four at primary school I entered a Jūdō competition hoping to beat the strongest fighter in my year, and won easily with Seoi-nage (shoulder throw), which gave my confidence a great boost. While at middle school I attended a boxing gym, and at high school I was active not only in Jūdō but also as a forward on the soccer team. At university I continued my Jūdō

The author receiving a certificate of appreciation from the FBI's training director. As he said, "fighting techniques which lack mental flexibility are of no use to us."

training at the Kōdōkan, and reached 5th Dan on merit alone. However, I began to feel that there was something missing in the sportified form of Jūdō, and started learning the techniques of old schools of martial arts, from a variety of teachers. After about ten years of this, I was privileged to meet Takamatsu Sensei, who had mastered nine schools of Budō. I then commuted to his house for fifteen years for his instruction.

Every week, I would leave Noda on Saturday, take an overnight train from Tōkyō and be treated to Sensei's teaching all through Sunday, returning from Kashihara (near Nara) on the Sunday night train. Back at home, I would bring myself to the 'zero point' where the self or ego no longer gets in the way, and do just as my lifelong master had told me, continuing to dedicate myself to intense practice. All the while, I could hear Sensei's words still echoing in my ears—"The true essence of the martial ways lies in virtue," "Martial arts are a path for perfecting yourself as a human being." Perfection demands persistence, and there is also a secret teaching in which perfection is mentioned with reference to seven lights, i.e.—the colors of a rainbow.

The first time I traveled abroad was in August 1982, to New York. I stayed there for one month, meeting many martial arts champions or highly graded practitioners from around the world who operated Dōjō there. When they all leapt on me I would lightly assist them to tumble over. This stunned them, and led them to recognize my ability. That is how I started teaching overseas.

With Raymond Ōtani, a swordwork grandmaster based in New York

As in this example, I never tried to subdue my opponents in fighting bouts or to boast of my victories. In Budō, how you express yourself is of great importance. Skilled Budōka can see through an opponent just by looking at them, assess their competence and understand what the result of a contest would be. That is why, if you meet an opponent stronger than yourself, you must transmit non-verbally (as if through telepathy) that "I cannot defeat you." If you cannot do this, then they are likely simply to slice you in two with their sword, or whatever weapons are at their disposal. Those who actually have fights and get killed are fools. Those who cannot say—as in the Samurai stories—"Sir, I perceive your ability to be quite outstanding" are not true martial artists.

Conversely, if you are strong, you should have the generosity to let the opponent know of your actual strength before such an encounter, and do your utmost to avoid any conflict. Even if it goes ahead and you win, avoid winning too overtly so that you can make the other side look good too. That is martial manners, the true way of a warrior.

TAIJUTSU WITH SHUKŌ

手鉤と体術

The Taijitsu (mysterious truth) of Shukō (plans) and Sokkō (execution)

TAIJUTSU WITH SOKKŌ

足鉤と体術

ITTŌ-DORI USING SHUKŌ

手鉤による一刀捕り

KIHON HAPPŌ GATA 基本八法型

The Kihon Happō consist of three Kosshi methods and five Torite methods. It is said that your martial arts will never be up to much if you are unable to master these Kihon Happō. It is also said that the myriad techniques of Budō were all borne from these eight basic techniques.

■ KOSSHI KIHON SANPŌ 骨指基本三法

FROM ICHIMONJI NO KAMAE
一文字の構えより

Position yourself in the stance Migi Ichimonji no Kamae: right arm extended, left fist and thumb upright as if placed on the elbow of the right arm.

FROM HICHŌ NO KAMAE

飛鳥の構えより

Turn right hand to the right, turning from hips to left shoulder. When turning, make the fist change. This is to destroy the enemy's attack.

FROM JŪMONJI NO KAMAE (OMOTE GYAKUDORI)

十文字の構えより（表逆捕り）

Think of Jūmonji not as the shape of the Japanese number ten, "十," but rather as "to join." This is Juppō Sesshō no Kamae.
Turn your left hand to the left and strike into the right side of the enemy's neck with a half-open fist; the left foot changes one step at the same time.

Takamatsu Sensei

FROM JŪMONJI NO KAMAE (URA GYAKUDORI)

十文字の構えより（裏逆捕り）

SHINOBI-ORI (OMOTE GYAKUDORI)

忍び折（面逆捕り）

1) Kyo/Jitsu—Omote Kote form. When the enemy grabs you on one side of your chest, raise your right hand high in Omote Kote-dori, pull back your right leg, and floor him by turning around the wrist.
2) Yin/Yang—Ura Kote form. When the enemy grabs you on one side of your chest and attempts to strike in with his right fist, receive this with your left fist. At the same time, take the enemy's left wrist in Omote Gyaku with your right hand, and throw as above.
3) Light/Dark—Ura Gyaku Ken-sabaki form. When the enemy grabs your chest, take his hand in Ura Kote-gyaku with your left hand, pull back your left leg, pull once below the Kote-gyaku, then immediately change. Turn the wrist from above, pull back your right leg, then throw him in line with your right hand.

SHINOBI-ORI (URA GYAKUDORI)

忍び折（裏逆捕り）

TAKE-ORI (GYAKUDORI)

武折（逆捕り）

The name can be interpreted as meaning to fracture and flatten a fierce warrior.

TAKE-ORI (GYAKUDORI)

猛折（逆捕り）

The name can be interpreted as meaning to fracture and flatten a ferocious fighter.

ONI-KUDAKI (OMOTE GYAKUDORI)

鬼砕（表逆捕り）

Take the elbow in this 'demon crusher'

ONU-KUDAKI
(URA GYAKUDORI)

隠砕き（裏逆捕り）

Take the elbow in this 'hidden crusher'

MUSHA-DORI

武者捕り

When the enemy takes your right sleeve in his left hand, pull your right arm to the right using a motion of your whole body. Put a lock on his arm by wrapping around him from above—be sure the movement is large enough. At the same time, kick a Kyūsho (pressure point, for example Sai, kaku or Yaku) on the enemy's right leg, and throw him so that he lands face up.

MUSŌ-DORI

無双捕り

The name implies flowing as in a dream.

GANSEKI-NAGE (PERFORM ON LEFT AND RIGHT)

巖石投げ

This can be seen as the basis of all throws. When the enemy takes your right sleeve with his left hand, pull back your right arm using a motion of your whole body, wrap in the enemy's left arm from the inside using your right hand, turn your left leg behind, and execute a Gyaku-nage.

TOGAKURE-RYŪ NINPŌ TAIJUTSU UKEMI-GATA
戸隠流忍法体術受身型

The important thing in these Taijutsu forms is that you remain free to attack or defend within the Ukemi. This awareness of Ukemi is quite different from that found in Jūdō or Aikidō: you can only learn the Ukemi-gata of Shinobi, survival-based Taijutsu once you know the Ukemi of the natural world.

KAESHI-DORI (RETURNING BIRD)
返し鳥

The opponent comes to cut in from Daijōdan (a position in which the sword is held over the head). The Ninja drops down, face up, then makes use of the reaction to kick up into the enemy's Suigetsu with both legs and return once again to his standing position.

KEN-NAGASHI

拳流し

The opponent comes to cut in with a Daitō from Daijōdan. Instantly strike into Suigetsu with a right, as if to make him fall face down, then turn, as if to make him fall in reverse, and stand.

YOKO-GERI (SIDE-KICK)

横蹴り

When the opponent comes to cut in from Daijōdan, do a side-kick with your right leg.

SEEN FROM A DIFFERENT ANGLE

Ichi no Kamae

一之構え

Ichi no Kamae ("The Stance of One") includes a stance of minus one, a stance of plus one, a stance of zero, and so on. This is connected with Juppō Sesshō no Jutsu.

Takamatsu Sensei

Sensei's hand in Ichi no Kamae

Ittō-dori (see following page)

一刀捕り

A poster of the famous ninja movie *Shinobi no Mono,* starring Ichikawa Raizō

ITTŌ-TORI—HICHŌ NO KAMAE

一刀鳳—飛鳥の構え

Hichō no Kamae emerges from Ittō-tori: a phoenix flies up from under the blade.

The opponent is in Daijōdan with a Daitō; your Kamae is reversed right/left. When the enemy cuts in, your left hand palm (palme d'or) receives it instantly, and your right hand soars straight to the enemy's face.

鹿嶋大神宮

KATATE-NAGE

肩手投げ

Katate-nage is usually written to mean "one arm throw," but it can also be interpreted as an instruction to throw using your shoulder, elbow and arm joints.

Picture by the author

Chapter

3

Ninja apparel

忍者の衣装

NINJA DRESS

When people talk of Ninja costume, they are normally referring to cloth dyed with sappanwood. That is because this color blends with the darkness. Shinobi would wear clothes with protective coloration, in other words, Shinobi colors that matched the environment—for Suiton, a watery blue; for Doton, earthy ochers; and for Setton, snow white. They would also employ different colors for the outside and inside of their clothes, and incorporate various tricks within the costume. As I mentioned in Chapter 1, Ninja garb was known as Ninniku Armor, showing an awareness of the Zen-like aspects of the Ninja code, i.e. to endure insults and discard grudges.

One day, I was asked, "What color is Shinobi color?" I answered immediately, "Rainbow-color of course, the colors of a prism. They blend with nature's colors, don't they? The colors of heaven, of earth, of humans, right? If you want to depict Ninjutsu, these are the colors you use, you paint with Shichihō Sanpō colors, colors used to disguise your thoughts!" A beautiful arc of red/orange/yellow/green/blue/indigo/violet—although it seems that these tones do not have universal currency outside Japan. I hear that the people in some countries regard the rainbow as five-colored or three-colored. If you get children around the world to draw rainbows, it is fascinating to observe how both the colors and shapes demonstrate infinite variety.

As I mentioned earlier above, there is a secret teaching in which perfection is described in terms of the 'seven lights,' i.e. a rainbow.

Sometimes this effect can be produced through multiple layers dyed with sappanwood. It is said that sappanwood was introduced to Japan during or before the Nara period (710–94), and was specified as the color to be used for the clothes of Nara government officials, which has interesting implications for Shinobi.

It is also said that clothes dyed with indigo protect you from poisonous snakes. In the Kamakura period (1185–1333), wearing an indigo suit of armor was regarded as a sure sign of victory, and so it came to be used as a 'winning color.' Later, in the Edo period, the beauty of the indigo hues in Hiroshige's (1797–1858) art was praised by people around the world as "Japan blue."

Shinobi also had something called "paper armor," which was used for disguise and

Clad in Ninja clothes

Shinobi-bukuro: a bag used by Ninja to carry the tools of their trade, which is hung from the waist.

A quilted coat as worn by Edo fire fighters, depicting the Ninja Orochi-maru. Used for Katon no Jutsu, and for both physical and metaphysical disguise.

evasion. Certain old documents refer also to the "armor of the four clans," saying, "the head of the Genji wore black, the Heike violet, the Fujiwara light green, and the Tachibana yellow." This means using colored armor for Hensō-jutsu—not merely techniques for changing one's appearance, but methods for changing the whole flow of battle. Kagemusha (the commander's doubles) would also wear this. Each section of armor would be inscribed with the names of protective deities and Kuji or Jūji spells.

WITHOUT THE SPIRIT OF YŪGEN THERE CAN BE NO BUDŌ

Japanese culture—including the martial arts—was perfected in the Muromachi period (1392-1568), particularly in the latter stages. One feature was that the culture of the common people surpassed that of the nobility, and this new culture thus became rooted in everyday life. Ikebana flower arranging, the Sadō tea ceremony, Nō drama, Buyō dancing, Sukiya-zukuri architecture, Kare-sansui gardens. . . what pervades all of these is the idea of "Yūgen"—a world of subtle, dark beauty. For example, photographs which are out of focus are more attractive because they have more "Yūgen-ness." If the photographer focuses carefully and takes a clear picture, in most cases they will end up with no more than an 'ordinary' result. That is why it is better to attach filters. You could say that it is better to create a form of wall, or barrier. Thinking about it, shields are a requisite part of life: the filters in photography function somewhat like shields themselves.

Human subjects too are conveyed better by the atmosphere they project, than by their body shape or facial features. The famous photographer Domon Ken (1909–90) once said, "When you are shooting photos, taking the subject itself is nothing special. In my case, if it's bamboo I take a 'likeness' of the bamboo, or if a woman, a 'likeness' of the woman." This 'likeness' is related to Yūgen. There may be Yin & Yang and the Goton aspects to a 'likeness' too, but if it is created through Yūgen, it becomes something truly wonderful. This can create out-of-the-box, extra-ordinary aesthetics within moving images too.

I think martial artists too only become genuine once they capture this 'likeness' and feeling of Yūgen. Conversely, those who ignore Yūgen and cannot be bothered to train end up as purely superficial, "imitation Budōka"—highly irritating and pretentious. The genuine Budōka treads far more lightly.

In former times, the Ninja would, if required, become itinerant actors or disguise themselves as patent medicine peddlers. Yet in Ninjutsu, disguise refers not so much to changing one's appearance as to changing one's thoughts. These "thoughts" really mean feelings, and concealed inside those feelings is the 'likeness' that the Ninja hopes to convey. The method resembles the Identikit pictures of criminals drawn up by police detectives. Apparently they start with the general shape of the face, but do not try to recreate it exactly—instead they draw a picture which conveys an atmosphere and feeling close to that of the criminal originally spotted. Pictures completed this way have a very high probability of leading to a successful arrest. This is another example of how the 'likeness' approach can get results.

Chain mail to be worn underneath a Ninja costume.
Made of iron rings interlaced on top of a cloth backing.

The Shinobi jacket has two inside pockets to carry Me-tsubushi, Shuriken, and the like.

1

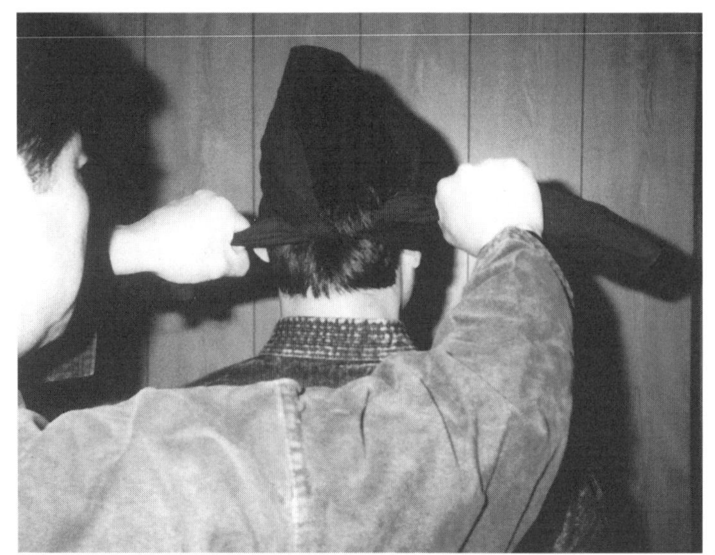
2

How to mask your face with Sanjaku-tenugui

1) Prepare two Sanjaku-tenugui (three-foot cloths). First cover your forehead with one of the cloths. . .
2) . . .then pass this to the back of the head, and tie it once. This is called "the top cloth knot."
3) Next, cover the lower part of your face with the second cloth (we have used a white one here to make it easier to see) as shown in picture 4, and again pass this to the back of the head.

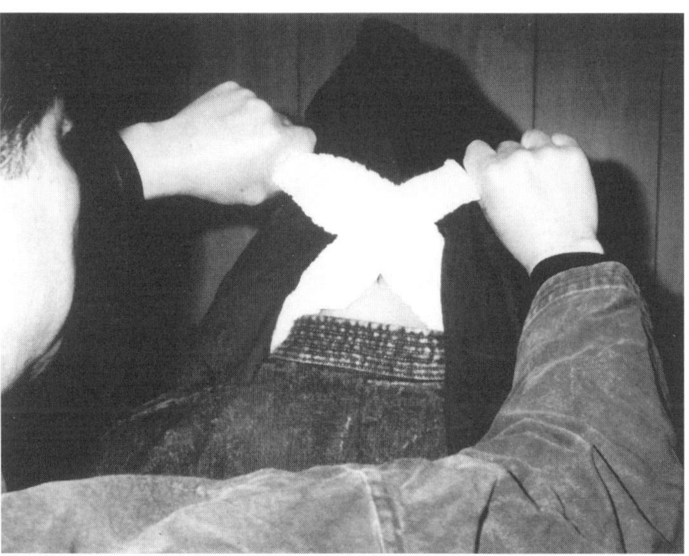
3

4

4) The top cloth must be positioned so that the Bushi coiffure can still protrude.

5) Now tie the lower cloth once on top of the top cloth knot, as shown at the bottom right of the illustration.

6) Finally, tie the top cloth once again on top of the lower cloth's knot. If you do this, the cloths will not fall off however much you move.

5

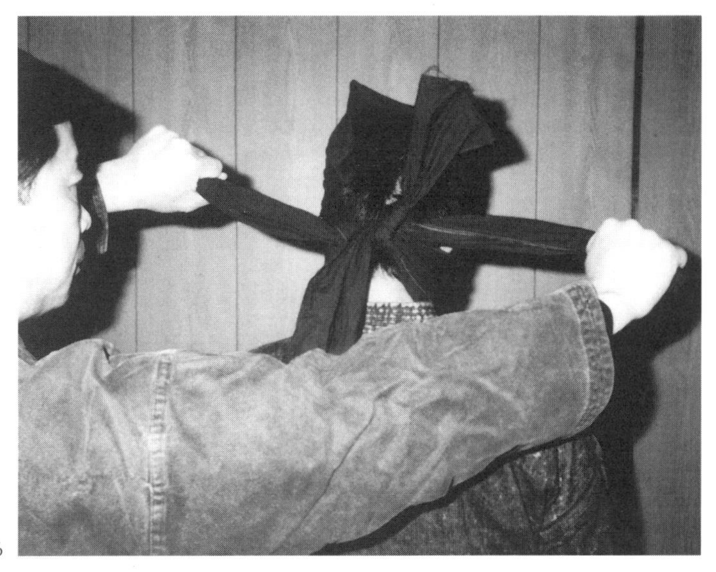

6

SEEN FROM THE FRONT

Even if the lower cloth is removed, the top cloth will not come free: your face remains securely masked. If a strong wind is blowing or the light is dazzling, you can cover your eyes with the top cloth. Even if the top cloth is pulled off backwards, the lower cloth mask will not fall. Also, if something gets dropped in front of you, producing smoke or a smell, you can cover your nose using the lower cloth. You can also protect yourself against noise by folding your ears over so that they guard your ear-holes, and covering them with the cloth.

Ankoku-tōshi no Jutsu: a method for seeing through the dark

暗黒透視術

Takamatsu Sensei

Ichikawa Raizō (on the set of *Shinobi no Mono*)

A snapshot of the author in the role of Yamaji Tetsuzan, Jiraiya's father in the TV series "Ninja Olympiad," which incorporated dynamic Ninja action. ▶

A Shinobi mask. Sanjaku-tenugui may also be used.

A chain-mail headpiece may also be worn underneath the mask.

Wearing chain mail in Ichi no Kamae. This would be worn underneath the Ninja costume. Alternatively, it might be concealed by other items of clothing if the Ninja were in disguise.

A Shinobi suit of armor made by Munechika of the Myōchin school

Ninja armor

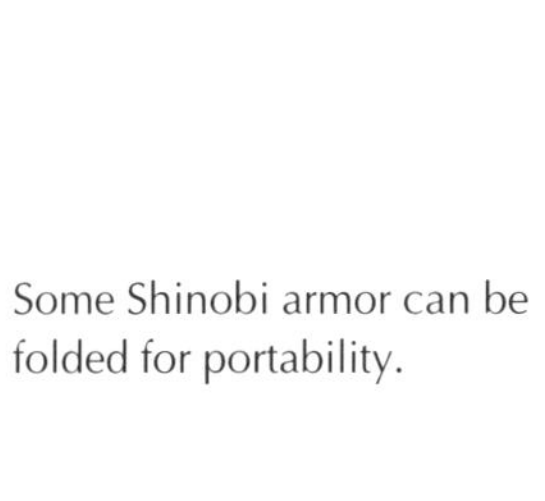

Some Shinobi armor can be folded for portability.

Fushin Manpozu: if it keeps going, even a pawn can be queened.

Chapter

4

Ninja training methods

忍者の訓練法

TAIJUTSU AND THE NINJA

Paul Klee (1879–1940), the Swiss painter who was a member of the Blue Rider group, said "Art does not reproduce the visible; rather, it makes visible." In the art of Ninpō Taijutsu too, it is important to cultivate the eyes of a god or Buddha so that you can perceive things which cannot normally be seen.

Takamatsu Sensei kindly told me the following words, expressing the attitude of a Ninja:

"What is endurance? It is the body of a Ninja. True Ninja are those who cultivate their spirit, train their technique, and persevere for time without end."

The French sculptor Auguste Rodin (1840–1917) said something quite similar:

"To create a masterpiece requires the perseverance of water dripping onto a stone."

In theory, no Ninja should lack skill in Ninpō Taijutsu, but the actual Taijutsu training differs from school to school. Having said this, all Ninja have to be equally agile and light in their movements. They also need to be excellent leapers. There are many methods for acquiring this leaping ability: Shihō-tobi (leaping in four directions), Asa-tobi (leaping in the early morning when the air is cleanest), and so on. Ninja would also wrap straw around a log and bind it firmly with cloth, then hit this pillar with their hands, fingers, and other striking parts or techniques in order to strengthen them. By such means they would fabricate a body, spirit, and striking ability beyond normal human limits, with the result that they could even split pebbles with their little finger.

The training additionally includes Shōten no Jutsu (tree climbing) and Sokusō-hō (rapid running), not to mention the practice of Taihenjutsu (techniques for changing the state of one's body). For example, if an enemy suddenly cuts in at you, you might escape in any of ten directions, or counterattack and deprive the enemy of his fighting spirit or weapon. If an enemy thrusts at you from behind, you might sense the energy of the attack, drop your body down to the side, roll, escape, and hide.

Before training, you should slap your whole body with the palms of your hands to stimulate the circulation. Next perform Jūnan-taisō, flexibility exercises—work on your mental and spiritual flexibility too.

A trainee is made to sit down with both legs extended, then encouraged to stretch forwards until flat, with the aid of a Kamayari spear. With his soles held together for stability, a stick is then placed across his thighs and pressed down, to help the hip joints become more supple. These exercises help promote flexibility in the neck, spine, hips, knees, ankles, and more.

METHODS OF TRAINING: ROPPŌ HOKŌ JUTSU, THE SIX WAYS OF WALKING

1) Walk on ice, run around, and practice Taihenjutsu—wearing Geta (clogs). This serves to give your body stability and balance, and teaches you how to walk silently.

2) Spend two hours every day walking with quick, small steps. Walking with small steps puts less strain on your heart. This also trains you for walking as if on a cushion of air, not letting your center of gravity rest on either leg.

3) Yoko-aruki: walking with your body sideways on. This type of leg movement is a feature of the Taijutsu in Kotō-ryū Koppō-jutsu.

4) Sokushin Sokusō-hō: adapt to a changed situation by practicing methods 1, 2, and 3 above at a running pace.

5) Learn the four ways of walking given above by watching the movements of famous dancers and soccer stars, or the Yūgen steps used in "Shimai" style Nō theater. My teacher taught me that Shinobi no Mono should always keep their feet warm. I remember how he used to wear Tabi even in summer. There is also a saying, "You can tell someone's art from their feet." A Zen parable states that, "Enlightenment lies under your feet," while there is also a proverb that teaches how having a cool head but warm feet is important for maintaining one's health. Oriental medicine asserts that there are fifty points on the feet, each connected to a different part of the body, and that the six energizing routes (the "six meridians") of the spleen, stomach, bladder, kidneys, liver, and gallbladder all pass through the feet. This all conveys the sense that it is important to keep one's feet warm and stimulate them correctly.

6) There is an art called Hensō Hokō-jutsu (disguised walking): one example would be walking with a stagger as if drunk. Another name for this is Yūgei Hokō-jutsu (the entertainer's walk).

ANYWHERE CAN BE A DŌJŌ IF THE SPIRIT IS RIGHT

When a child is born, nobody consciously teaches it to walk or feed itself; rather these things occur instinctively. Human beings are born with almost limitless capabilities and functions, and we really should make greater use of them. For example, if a child could develop the power to think for itself, even without attending school, and studied from computers or the TV, it would become far more intelligent than the students who nowadays gain entrance to the top universities. Why should everyone attend school in an identical fashion? I have no doubt that sometime in the future, schools will become superfluous—those that have been built so far are no more than money exchanges.

Studying for oneself and making one's own discoveries is much more important

SEIZA

正坐

While the trainee is sitting in Seiza, a sword is gradually brought down close in front of him to make him fall backwards.

When visiting Tucson, Arizona, a miraculous rainbow appeared to greet me.

Holding the world's top sniper rifle

than group learning, and this applies equally well to the martial arts. Of course, nothing beats attending a Dōjō and rigorously training there under a master; but even if you do not attend a Dōjō and simply continue training by yourself, provided you do this with a sincere spirit, that place will become a Dōjō. As I often say, "Life is all about solitary training." This is because I want serious practitioners to discover the tricks of the trade for themselves.

The world is not made up solely of good people—nor of bad people alone, either. It is quite natural that there are good and bad Budōka too. Each individual is different. I was fortunate that such a wonderful person as Takamatsu Sensei still existed, so that I could learn from him how people ought to live. Having a true heart is so important for human beings. Above all, it is important to be able to maintain this right until the end, until the day you die.

Kon Tōkō (1898–1977), a novelist who also became the abbot of Chūsonji temple, once gave me some calligraphy with the words "A true heart: this is the Dōjō." I too have a cherished motto, "Ninpō Ikkan, Magokoro ni Masare" (persistence in Ninpō: a just spirit in a true heart).

To become strong, powerful, or famous is really nothing special. People who seek seriously for a martial art with integrity, and having found it never leave it, are the protectors of true Ninjutsu and Ninpō Taijutsu. People who can really devote themselves to the genuine martial arts are trustworthy members of society too. They possess a spirit of self-criticism, gratitude, and sincerity.

In this respect, let me also say that a true master in the martial ways has a heart of beneficence, and will share his art with anyone he encounters, regardless of whether they are a student of his or not. This does not just apply to those who are somehow connected to him, but to anyone who comes within his circle.

At an exhibition of my sketches in the Gallery at the Lowry Hotel, Manchester

THE NINJA DIET

It is said that humans have grown weaker since we started to eat cooked food. Shinobi no Mono would normally eat unpolished, brown rice, but white rice when fighting. This is not simply because white rice is easier to digest but it also stems from the fact that white was seen as a symbol of victory.

While the martial arts contain Omote ("straightforward") techniques and Ura ("dark side") techniques, the Ninja diet has three sides to it: Omote, Ura, and the Void. The Ura technique encourages the practitioners to fill the Void with anything they can, and to eat unbalanced, strange, possibly 'disguised' food. Leading a deliberately irregular life also helps you to cultivate a sense of balance for different time zones (like those on shift work). When undercover, Ninja might spend long periods unable to soak up the sun, and they would therefore also train in being "night owls." Ordinary people tend to regard such unorthodox lifestyles as indicating failure, but the Ninja were in control of their own lives, and their spiritual powers of endurance helped them perfect the skills needed to transform the unconventional into commonplace activities. Whenever I travel around the world giving guidance in Ninpō Taijutsu, I never have any problems with jet lag or unusual food. Unlike many, I actually relish such experiences.

Having a healthy everyday diet is still the foundation on which one should build the kind of body which will help one's Taijutsu grow. Above all, I recommend eating plenty of vegetables. The Ninja Kihon Happō diet consists of brown rice, tōfu, sesame, miso soup, no salt, no sugar, uncooked food, and colored vegetables. The brown rice can be roasted on a stone using sunlight. The other important thing is to eat everything, without preference or fussiness. Moreover, you should enjoy your food—and chew it well. This is useful for recovering from mental and physical fatigue.

Soldiers at war used to be fed military rations whose three principal constituents were

Following the Ninja diet helps develop a body suitable for Taijutsu.

soya beans, brown rice, and pickled plums. Soya beans in particular are known as the "warrior's food" or "magic food," as they can be transformed into miso, soya sauce, and tōfu. In recent years, people all over the world have started using soya sauce and eating tōfu and brown rice, possibly because they have recognized this principle.

THOUGHTS ON THIRTY-THREE

In Kyōto there is a famous building called the Sanjūsangendō (Thirty-three bay hall). It is the main hall of the Tendai sect's Rengeōin. It was first built by Taira no Kiyomori (1118–81) at the behest of the retired Emperor Goshirakawa (1127–92), and is famous for its 1,001 statues of the Thousand-handed Kannon. The Hannya Shingyō (heart sutra), which distills the essence of Buddhism into a mere 262 Chinese characters, is the shortest Buddhist scripture, having been translated into Chinese by the monk Xuanzang (602–64), also famous as the model for Sanzang in "Journey to the West" (a.k.a. "Monkey"). This sutra describes how Kannon reaches the world of enlightenment, and has from ancient times been widely recited by lay believers as well as the priesthood. Kannon has been a popular focus of faith. She is said to be able to change form at will into thirty-three different aspects, and to have great compassion and mysterious wisdom, stretching out her hands to the masses seeking salvation. There are thirty-three bays between the pillars of this hall, which is the origin of the name. Like Kannon, Ninja too change their appearance in thirty-three ways, and have a mission to protect life, nations, people, and their own clan and family.

By a bizarre coincidence, Takamatsu Toshitsugu Sensei was appointed the head and "top Tengu" of Kumano Shugendō at the age of thirty-three, and subsequently became the 33rd grandmaster of the Togakure school. I in turn received my Menkyo Kaiden in the Ninpō Taijutsu of Togakure-ryū etc. on "an auspicious day in March, in the 33rd year of the Shōwa period"—and this book is being published to mark the 33rd anniversary of Takamatsu Sensei's death. It is quite mysterious. In some areas it is said that after the 33rd anniversary of someone's death, they become a divine being; a Kami.

Thousand-handed Kannon statues in the Sanjūsangendō, Kyōto

ROPPŌ HOKŌ JUTSU—WALKING THE SIX WAYS
六方歩行術

When I take our many dogs for a walk, I walk quickly with small steps. Suddenly a cat appears—or is it the dog's mortal enemy, a monkey? Sometimes three leads all pull in the same direction, sometimes each pulls in a different direction, sometimes it's two against one. I use Sabaki to balance gravity against levity, and control the three sets of leashes and legs.

It is said that if you pay reverence to Idaten, a swift-running heavenly warrior, you will become a strong runner and never want for food.

Mythical three-legged crow

The author with a famous Argentine dancer. The footwork of the tango is similar to that used in Budō.

Ninja walking

SHINOBI STEPS

忍び足並みの法

The Ninja would study various gaits, including stealthy steps, shuffling steps, skipping steps, small steps, large steps, tight steps, hopping steps, mincing steps, crawling steps, disguised steps, and normal steps.

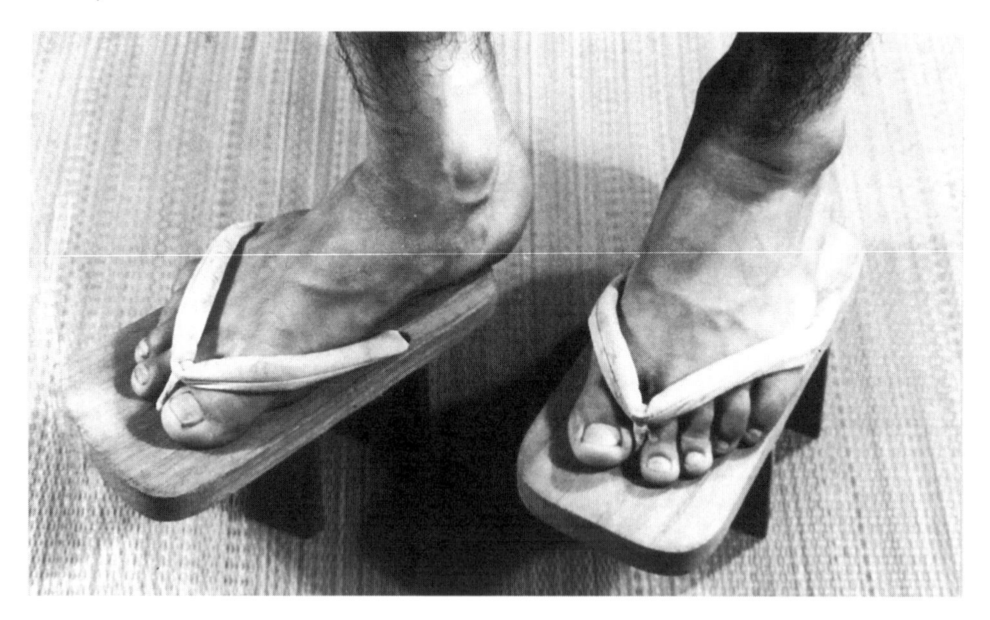

TEARING ALONG THE MUNDANE TRAIL

地門がけ

TRAINING TO RUN FAST FORWARD, FLEET OF FOOT
速進速足法

Ninja practice breathing through the nose, through the mouth, and not at all.

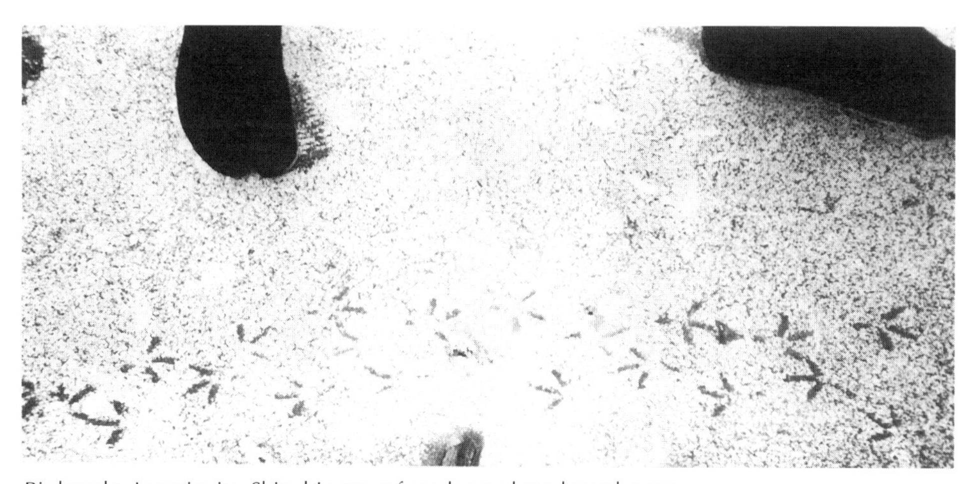

Bird tracks. In antiquity, Shinobi were referred to as three-legged crows.

GETA TAIJUTSU

下駄体術

Taijutsu includes Geta Taijutsu (this is a Kuden). It is said that the Eskimo also run across the ice with small steps.

Ninja walk on ice wearing Geta to improve their balance for Ninpō Taijutsu movements. It is also good practice for Taijutsu, fighting when wearing Geta, and using different ways of walking to send signals.

Practicing Tate-nagare, Yoko-nagare, Zenpō-ukemi, Sutemi-gata on the ice. Be aware that these too are forms of walking: it is the whole body that walks, not merely the feet.

In seasons when there is no ice, Ninja train their balance by scattering beans or spreading wax on the Dōjō floor to make it slippery, and practicing there, wearing Tabi.

YOKO-ARUKI: SIDE STEPS WALKING FREELY TO RIGHT AND LEFT

横歩き
左右自由歩き

In Yoko-aruki you swing your arms to and fro and use your fingers to balance your legs as you walk freely to either side.

Yoko-aruki, Yoko-kamae, Yoko-aruki. This is also known as Sanshin Aruki.

A Yoko-aruki

B Yoko-kamae

C Yoko-aruki

HIDING IN THE MIST (MUTON NO JUTSU), WITH SEEKING STEPS (SAGURI-ARUKI)

霧遁の術　探り歩き

Yoko-aruki can also be used as a form of Taijutsu: Ninja exploit the Kamae of Taijutsu and practice walking in a way which leaves no openings.

HŌKO NO KAMAE: THE 'SURROUNDING' STANCE

包囲の構え

Ninja must change freely between Hōko no Kamae and Ichi no Kamae. If you walk in the Jūmonji way, in tune with the gods, the very space you are in also holds a Kamae.

A

B

C

OTO-ARUKI: SOUND STEPS

音歩き

Many people think that Ninja walk silently, but that is not so. There are Yō-nin (overt subterfuge) steps where you do make a noise as you walk. With Goton and Tenchijin, that makes thirty different methods of walking.

IWA-ARUKI

岩歩き

Rather than "climbing" castle walls, a Ninja makes his body stick close to the stones and "walks" across them like a lizard. This is Chūton: the art of the centipede.

OKUTON HOKŌ JUTSU—EVASIVE ROOF WALKING

屋遁歩行術

Ninja use human platforms to avoid making any sound.

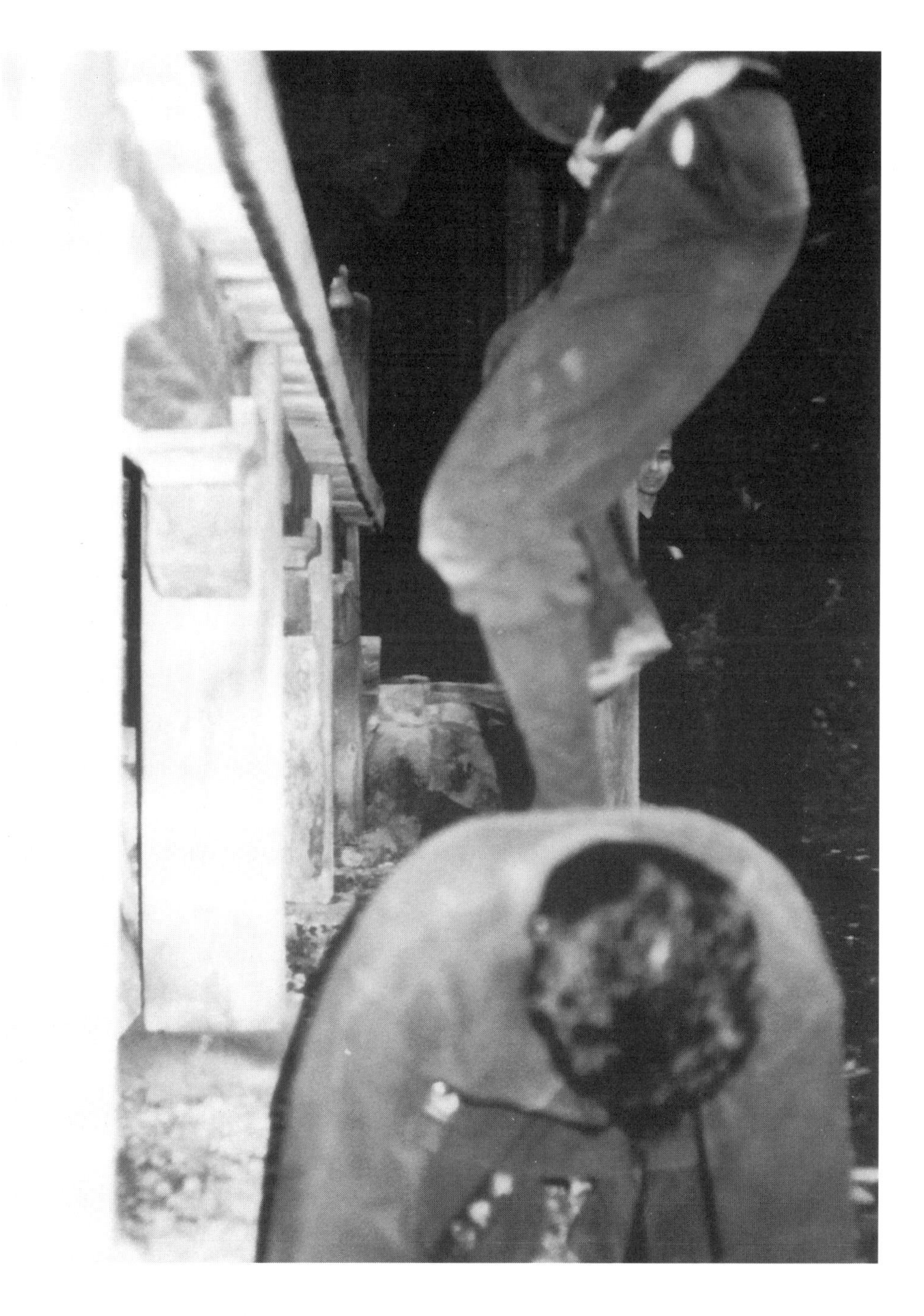

SHINOBI-ARUKI

忍び歩き

Within the martial arts, Shinobi walking is classified into Sabaki, Shirabe, and Moguri steps: action, exploration, and evasion.

FREESTYLE

自由型

Free forms change depending on the environment, Tenmon and Chimon. Run like the wind, like the deity Idaten.

KŌTON: LIGHT EVASION

光遁

At times a Ninja shows his presence while advancing or retreating.

TONSŌ NO JUTSU

遁走の術

East West South North Up Down: 6 directions + Kyojitsu = 6x6; 36 methods of escape, Tonsō no Jutsu. The mystical power of six-way Kuji.

REVOLVER

回転型

If you watch the timing as the sword cuts in, you can flip over the top.

SCIENCE SHOULD PLAY SECOND FIDDLE TO NINJUTSU

A certain "Ninjutsu researcher" once said, quite seriously, "I intend to analyze Ninjutsu scientifically." I immediately retorted "You must be crazy!" There are still so many unknowns in science. Moreover, if one considers whether or not what has been done in the name of science has been for the good of mankind, the answer is not an unqualified 'yes.' Nor has it been for the good of nature. We need to confront these issues directly. Science has a lot to answer for, from the invention of dynamite to the development of weapons of mass destruction such as the atomic bomb. It is what defines the history of our modern world. Ninjutsu, in contrast, has not committed such errors; Ninja understood all along that science was a demonic art which altered the nature of things. The Ninja always concentrated on the relationship between heaven, earth, and man, and lived in accordance with natural providence. A Ninja's duty is surely to sneak into the world of science, and ensure that it is the servant, not the master. Do you not agree?

AERIAL TURN

空転

Free Taihen

Shinobi swimming through space

By knowing the limits of their own jumping prowess, and the turning points or essential elements of any situation, Ninja become able to make full use of their tools, as well as their environment and the nature around them. That is the most important thing to remember.

By cultivating an aerial feeling, you can learn astral projection.

FLYING WITH HITEN NO JUTSU

飛天の術

SHŌTEN NO JUTSU

昇天の術

Running straight up a cedar tree

Shōten no Jutsu refers to the art of running up pillars, partitions, and various kinds of obstacles. Ninja start training in this art by placing a board approximately 2 inches wide and 4 yards long at an initial angle of 45°, and practicing running up it in a single spurt. Once they have accomplished this, they progress to 50°, 60°, and finally 90°.

SPRING OF LIFE 飛生

Leaping around in all directions—the four compass points, the eight intermediate directions, and then high and low.

HIKŌ JUTSU: FLYING

飛行術

Hikō Jutsu, which is one form of Taijutsu, includes jumps very close to the ground called Shihō Tobi (literally, leaping in four directions). There is also Tenchi-tobi, consisting of upward leaps (Ten) and downward drops (Chi).

Hichō Tenmon Chimon Tobi

Slicing through the waves with the flying cut of Tengu Tobi-kiri Nami-kiri no Jutsu. The rolling motion of a ship can be used to assist jumping.

Leaping into space through darkness and light

Leaping from tree to tree like a monkey

Chuang Tzu's "wooden fighting-cock." In this Taoist parable, a fighting-cook was trained so well that it appeard totally impassive (wooden), thus inspiring terror in all its rivals.

Chapter

5

Hidden teachings of Ninpō Taijutsu

秘伝忍法体術

THE PHILOSOPHY OF NINJUTSU IS UNIVERSAL

The philosophy of Ninjutsu is universal—in fact, one could say that Ninjutsu itself is a universal system.

Theories that the mother of mankind, "Eve," lived in Africa, have become widely accepted as a result of mitochondrial DNA analysis. As mankind flowed from Africa to the four corners of the globe, the various tribes learned many different things. The religions that arose in this way—Christianity, Buddhism, Islam, etc.—are again quite diverse, but the same, single human race is at the root of them all. They simply changed to match the local environment and people. Instead of getting caught up in the differences between them, we should learn the essence of global culture, which flows in common through all regions. This essence has much in common with Ninjutsu; the important thing is to discover and learn it based on Juppō Sesshō no Jutsu.

The core of Ninjutsu is a third way, which offers homage to both religious and martial ways—or 'winds,' as sometimes expressed (in some cultures the wind is seen as the supreme deity). Recently, I feel that I have at last become able to see this with the eyes of homage, or perhaps with my "third eye." The basis of all life is duality and the unity thereof: the Yin and Yang principle. If both aspects are not present, it is unsteady, just like a family, whose fundamental unit is a couple, man and wife. The human body too has both arteries and veins, carrying 'red' blood and 'blue' blood. Human life depends on two complementary channels. The combination of two gives birth to future life, just as a man and wife produce a child. Having said this, it can be fatal to assume that this is a hard-and-fast rule, forgetting that Yin and Yang might reverse positions or split apart, depending on the environment, people, time, place, and circumstances. That is why you need to go one step further.

Ninjutsu contains deep wisdom, but it also contains many aspects that would be dangerous if learned by the general public. It is after all an art for controlling people, and on occasion snatching their swords and spears—figuratively, their will to fight—before escaping. It is also a way of controlling oneself and one's opponents. Living and dying, the taking and the granting of life are all connected. Strength and weakness are interlinked, Yin and Yang are part of one chain. It is important to recognize this. It

Takamatsu Sensei. You have to be on your guard with smokers, as they can blow the smoke from their cigarette into your eyes.

Teaching Koshi-tsubo techniques

Teaching Te-makura techniques

doesn't matter how strong you might be, there is absolutely no way you can survive on strength alone. Also, if someone definitely needed to win and survive, then no matter how weak they might be, they could use these techniques to control—or overpower—their opponents. That is what the martial arts are all about.

As I have discussed, Ninjutsu is the "art of escaping" (see page 30), and the truths above are well demonstrated by the proverb "discretion is the better part of valor." One might also say that it offers better value.

Studying the martial arts implies learning these truths, and living with the danger of life and death, the taking and granting of life. To do this, you have to have greater knowledge and understanding of life than other people, and persevere with the will to become a person who invites peace through their own virtue, not through fighting. For that reason alone, it is vital in Budō to observe the trends of the age well, and decide when to endure and when to act.

Hagakure, a transcription of the words of the Saga Samurai Yamamoto Tsunetomo (1659–1721), is well known for the phrase "The way of Bushi is the way of death." Many people who read this concluded that the ultimate truth of Bushidō is to die a magnificent death for the sake of one's lord, either in battle or through suicide following the lord's death. When I hear those words, a faint memory from my youth comes back to me. One day, a pet cat I was very fond of suddenly disappeared. This cat had sensed its own death approaching, and searched out a place to die where its master would not find it. At that moment, I remembered a scene from Kipling's *The Jungle Book*, where a gigantic elephant prescient of its own demise heads off through the moonlight towards the elephants' graveyard.

It is not just elephants and cats: many members of the animal world sense death approaching and quietly search for a place to expire. Bushi and Ninja are always prepared to offer their lives for the sake of their lord or village, and die serenely. It is a wonderful way to live. All worldly things are impermanent; life and death are but one. Bushidō is what runs through the Wabi and Sabi (transient beauty) of nature. Yet I feel compelled to say that enduring to the end no matter what happens, persevering with life despite being prepared for death at any time, is actually the secret of Bushidō. This means treasuring the lifestyle of the Ninja, living as a shadow of your true purpose, and doing your utmost to survive.

There is a secret martial arts Densho called "Neko no Myōjutsu" ("The Cat's Eerie Skill"), written by Issai Chozan, which contains the following fable. A certain swordsman was plagued by the presence of a large rat in his house. He tried to get his pet cat to catch it, but it lost the confrontation and returned in tears. Next he released some cats from the neighborhood, each of which gave the appearance of being exceptionally tough, but they all came running back with their tails between their legs. Finally he recalled that some six or seven blocks away there lived an unusual, aged cat, and went to borrow it. This cat strolled in at quite a leisurely pace, yet the strong rat cowered and was caught without any difficulty. In order to understand this story, it is important to realize that the cat was not simply light on its feet: it had Heijōshin, it had mastered the

SHINOBI-GAESHI GATA: SHINOBI COUNTERS 忍び返し型

Shinobi counters are used when Ninja perform Shinobi techniques, when their techniques are discovered, or when they deliberately reveal their techniques as a ploy. When a Ninja is in hiding—hiding his body, his art, and his heart—close encounters with the unknown may cause a flash of Shinobi inspiration to be transformed into a Shinobi counter-technique. One can savor a strange sense of the cycle of rebirth in this process.

Shige-gaeshi
While near the wall of a mansion, an enemy approaches from in front. The Ninja puts both hands on the wall, and while placing his left elbow on top, uses the reaction of pulling his right hand to swing his body lightly up and assume a prone position on the wall.

Shige-tori
The Ninja has assumed a prone position as described above; as soon as the enemy approaches the wall, he swings his body lightly to its previous position, kicks the enemy's face with both feet, then turns and leaps inside the wall.

principle of life and death, and it knew where the dying spot was.

It is easy to see why Takamatsu Sensei chose Mōroku ('Senility') as a nom de plume for some of his whimsical sketches.

A NINJA'S VIEW OF THE UNIVERSE

When people talk of the universe, many speak of things that are quite absurd, such as the fact that the average distance of the earth from the sun is 149,600,000 km, or that the boundary of the perceptible universe is approximately fifteen billion light-years away. In my opinion, the universe and human beings are connected: that's all there is to it. I think you obtain a much truer view of the universe by stating actual perceptions, commenting on how beautiful it is to see a crescent moon peering between the clouds, or talking of how gloomy the overcast sky is today, and how pleasant the weather is after a storm. The secret is to let your own existence resonate with the universal consciousness, and think of the universe that way.

It is so important to feel an emotional or sensory engagement. Scientists and researchers keep changing their theories, about the universe as well as other things. Views on how literature ought to be read and interpreted change just as frequently. People's needs change too, from time to time. Thus, many scholars are unable to determine what is genuine, where the truth lies. If you persevere in Ninjutsu as I have done, you will come to discern the ocean of difference that lies between things seen with true eyes, observed using the intuitive "feeling" you develop in this art, and those seen through the glass eyes of people who have not trained at all.

FLYING THROUGH THE AIR

空飛

A Ninja would leap onto the lowest bough, then bounce above it. Making use of the reactive force, he next uses his left hand to leap up onto the second branch. The second his legs reach a stable place between two branches, he uses his right hand to throw some Shuriken.

YOKO-NAGARE (SIDE FLOW)

横流れ

Sensing the moment when the opponent is about to attack—the moment when his killing intention reaches its peak—I launch a full Kiai at him, together with Metsubushi from my right hand (this is a shadow Kiai, executed when you feel as one with nature), and drop down as I turn sideways to the left. Placing my weight on my right leg, I turn and fall. (Anyone can do this noisily; the secret is to train so that you can do it silently.)

CHŪ-GAERI

中返り

As the enemy approaches from behind, I execute a silent Chū-gaeri to the front. In the initial stages it is fine to do this with your hands touching the ground, but you have to train so that you can do the turn freely without any hand contact.

It is important to note that Chū-gaeri is written here not the conventional way, as a "mid-air roll" but with characters indicating a roll "in the middle." Changes occur in the midst of life.

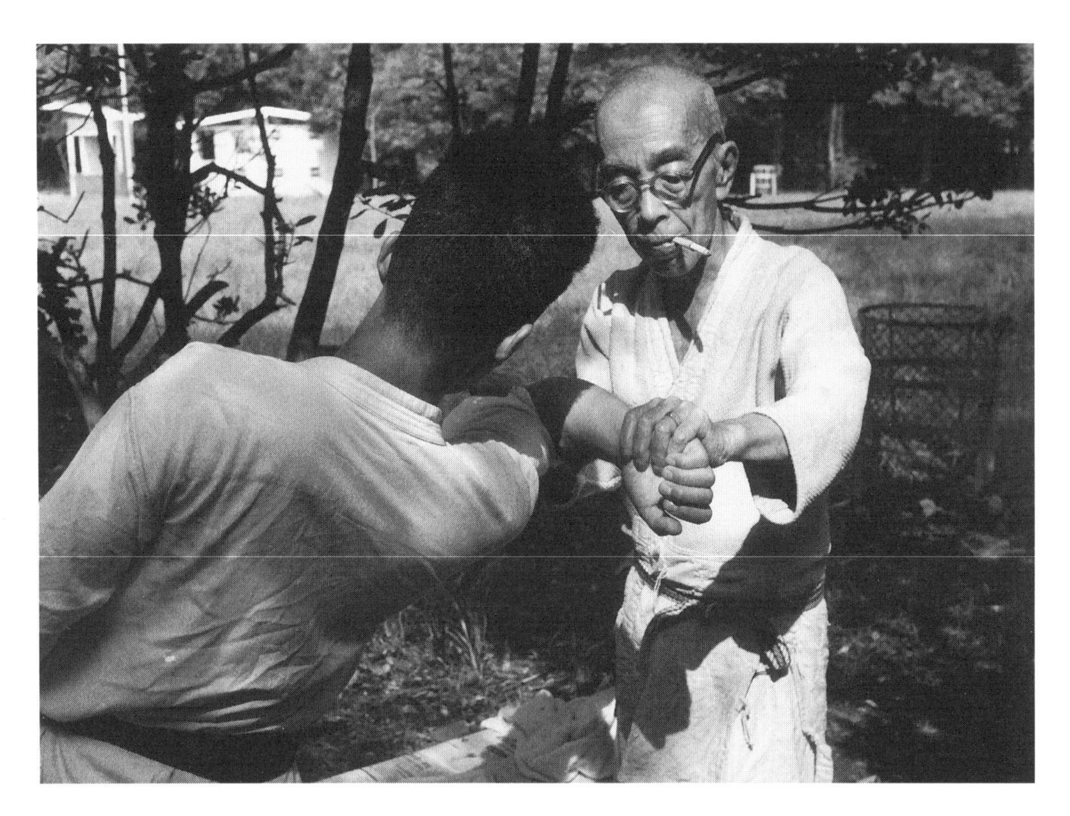

Learning Gyaku-te from my teacher

TEPPAN-NAGE→SENBAN-NAGE

鉄盤投→銛盤投

I place nine Teppan (thin iron plates) on my left hand, take them one by one with the right hand, and throw them horizontally forwards from the left side, thinking about the relative positions of my right wrist and the enemy in front. The intention is to throw them by means of my wrist movement. When practicing this move, you start off using business cards.

KIRI-KAESHI

切返

If you and your opponent are in equivalent positions relative to each other and to your swords, you should always move to the Naka-Seigan stance, and when the enemy cuts in, match their Kiai by stretching out, reversing your wrist and cutting back at their body. This is the "secret sword."

Simply thrust in. Throw the sword as if into a board, then cut to the side.

SUTEMI: SELF-SACRIFICE

捨身

If your enemies are many, the only route open to you may be one of Sutemi, but ensure that you move in as if making a true, straight thrust at their leader. The deceptive strategy (Kyojitsu) is to cut into the weakest people among them, break through their cordon, and escape by using Sutemi again in a similar fashion. That is the Ninja way of handling such situations.

Sutemi also contains a sense of moving as though empty handed, even while holding a sword.

TOGAKURE-RYŪ NINJA JŪNI-GATA, SANTŌ TONKŌ NO KATA

戸隠流忍者十二型、竄逃遁甲の型

These Kata are a mixture of Ninpō Taijutsu and Tongyō forms, and were created for training beginners in Ninpō. When preparing for a demonstration, you should add two pockets to the inside left of each Shinobi costume, and in the pockets conceal Metsubushi and practice (i.e. wooden or card) Senban Shuriken.

Sensei telling me, "This is how you make it!"

ONE-ARM TONSŌ-GATA

片腕遁走型

Leaving my right hand in the opponent's grasp, I take one, then two steps together with him, pulling in closer. On the third step, I take the opponent's right wrist in Take-ori from the palm side, as shown in the photograph, and lift his right hand high. With that motion, I kick into his lower area with my right leg. Then, keeping the Take-ori on the opponent's right wrist, in other words, guiding him via the Take-ori lock, I turn round on his right side. The turning Sabaki (motion) and the Take-ori enable me to take his elbow and shoulder joints, guide his body, and send him flying in Katate-nage.

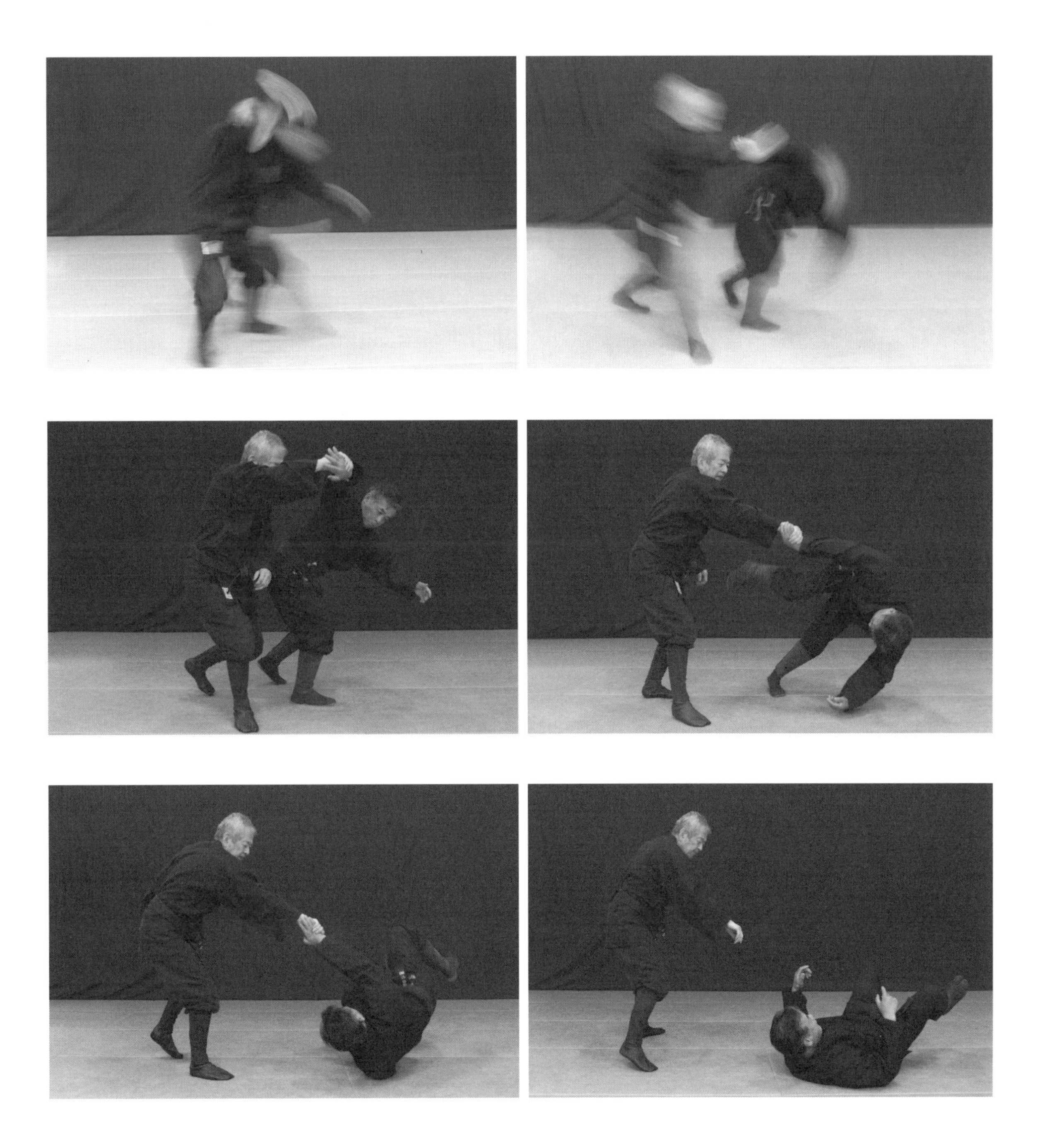

LEFT/RIGHT TONSŌ-GATA

左右遁走型

AS TAUGHT BY THE MASTER

The opponent holds my left wrist with his right hand, and tries to pull me in and grab me. After he has pulled me three steps, I take his right wrist in Take-ori using my left hand, take his right arm with my right hand, kick into his lower area with my right leg, and floor him face-down. Right Tonsō-gata is the same except that the opponent holds my right wrist with his left hand.

NECK TONSŌ-GATA

首筋遁走型

The master teaching

ART AND THE NATURE OF GENIUS

Think of an artist with true genius: many people would probably offer the names of Pablo Picasso (1881–1973) or Henri Matisse (1869–1954). However, Picasso could never be anything other than Picasso, and Matisse could only ever be Matisse. That is the destiny of a genius. The interesting thing is that such people did not consider themselves geniuses. They also lived as they pleased, free and easy-going. This is surely quite significant. The same applies to the martial arts. Some people of course jump to the conclusion that they themselves possess the attributes of a genius, especially when they are on a high. The interesting thing here, though, is that for some of them, the mere belief that they are a genius functions as a source of energy so that they actually produce works worthy of such a genius.

The talents of a genius may seem to change and gain value over time. A truly great genius only appears once every few centuries. This is because much depends on the natural characteristics with which they are born. Japanese arts such as the tea ceremony, Ikebana flower arranging, Nō drama and the like were established by geniuses, and then inherited under the Iemoto ('head of the house' = Sōke) system. Some people now say that the Iemoto system should be abolished, but truly dedicated, good Iemoto have preserved the techniques and forms of the original genius, and deserve just recognition for this. This is also the reason that certain lineages of the martial arts contain entries reading "xxx generations abbreviated": certain Sōke were not of sufficient quality to be listed.

Doton
土遁

RIGHT-HAND NECK TONSŌ-GATA

右手首筋遁走型

The opponent uses his right hand to feel my collar, trying to make me stop. He tries to pull me in, and while I move backward one step, then a second step, I let my right hand float on the hand that is pulling. The feeling is that I am making the opponent float in the flow of my technique. Then I strike the opponent's Suigetsu (the solar plexus) with my left elbow, firmly apply a Gyaku-dori, and, while carefully controlling the balance between his right wrist and elbow joint, perform Katate-nage.

ATE-KOMI TONSŌ-GATA

当込遁走型

AS TAUGHT BY THE MASTER

The opponent's Daitō is in Daijōdan. I lower my hips, and form a Shutō (knife-hand) with my left hand, with the right hand extended straight out behind, knuckles near the right shoulder. I am in Hachimonji no Kamae (arms raised in the shape of "八," the Kanji for "eight"), with my fingers pointing upwards. After launching a Kiai into the opponent, I leap just in front of him, floor him with a right thumb strike into Suigetsu, then jump to the right.

ATE-KOMI TONSŌ-GATA ON TWO OPPONENTS

二人当込遁走型

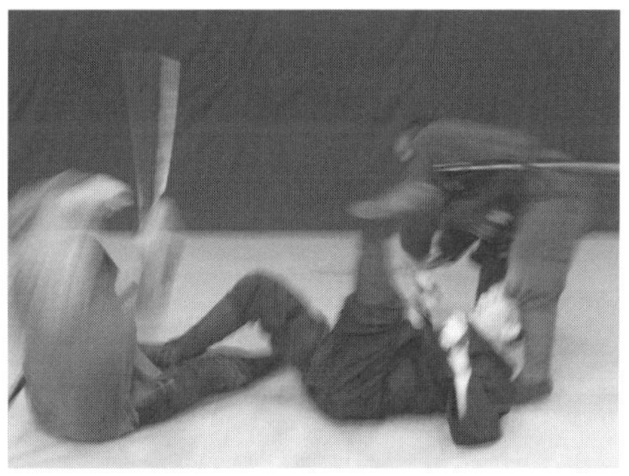

SEEN FROM A DIFFERENT ANGLE

KOTE-UCHI TONSŌ-GATA

小手打遁走型

AS TAUGHT BY THE MASTER

The opponent's Daitō is in Daijōdan; I am in Hachimonji no Kamae. When the opponent cuts in with his sword, I avoid it by shifting to the left, and hit his upper arm with a right Shutō. The enemy drops his sword, and I strike my left fist into the ribs on his right side. Then I leap to the left and execute Mokuton.

Mokuton
木遁

RIGHT STRIKE TONSŌ-GATA

右打遁走型

The opponent's Daitō is in Seigan no Kamae; I am in Happō no Kamae. The opponent thrusts in with a full Kiai. I turn my body to the right, strike the opponent's left upper arm with my right Shutō, grab the end of the sword with my left hand and pull it off him, then leap to the right and execute Mokuton.

LEFT/RIGHT KUMOGAKURE-GATA

左右雲隠型

Enemies approach from left and right in Daijōdan, from around four yards away. I am in Happō-gakure no Kamae with both my fists clenched; unknown to them, each hand holds Metsubushi. Happō-gakure is a stance with a low hip position, both hands just above your head, and your knees wide apart. The opponents come straight in and try to cut at me. I edge backwards two or three times, then instantly fire both Metsubushi. Immediately afterwards I leap in, strike them using both fists, and perform Chū-gaeri twice to the front before concealing myself with Mokuton.

Know in advance the number of people in the assignment

KŌSEI KIRIGAKURE-GATA

攻勢霧隠れ型

Four opponents try to attack with Daitō from about five yards in front. They approach in Seigan Jōdan; I am in Tonsō no Kamae. Tonsō is a stance indicating an intention to flee backwards, with the right leg in front and the body turned to the left, although "backwards" can also be written with Kanji implying a "crossover way." In my left hand I hold just the right number of Teppan for the people and duties that await me. The enemies fall for it and attack. Immediately I throw the Shuriken. While the enemies flinch, I leap in, scatter Metsubushi, and perform Chū-gaeri between the enemies in front of me before concealing myself with Mokuton.

Tonsō no Kamae

Initially, instead of putting your hands on the ground, burrow through in Moguri-gata.

NINJA ADVICE ON MARTIAL ARTISTRY

It is a great shame for me to watch the poor quality of martial arts consultancy and choreography in recent years. Bugeisha/Ninja have to have knowledge in all fields. The world of the theater, films, and music taught me a lot about the moving image, and gave me a wide range of experiences which have stood me in very good stead. I have acted as martial arts consultant to many theatrical and film productions, and offered acting guidance too. The advice I provided to the producers or actors was often a 'raw diamond,' and the end result turned into a masterpiece or a failure depending on how well they studied and polished what they had been given.

One of them was hailed a masterpiece of the Ninja genre, and was also serialized: *Shinobi no Mono* (1962; directed by Yamamoto Satsuo, starring Ichikawa Raizō, based on the book by Murayama Tomoyoshi). In this there was one scene in which the actor Itō Yūnosuke (playing the part of Momochi Sandayū, head of the Iga-ryū Ninja) had to race across the screen. When I asked him to use normal Ninja motions, the result was not at all interesting. But when I had him run with the feeling that his bladder was about to burst. . . it became a movement any Ninja would have been proud of! We all laughed at how important "endurance" was.

When acting as a Ninja arts consultant, I sometimes embed codes into the script that ordinary people would never be able to recognize. Although there are no preordained rules for these codes, the key elements are dotted throughout the space. In other words, I blend the forms (actually, the essence of the forms) with realistic portrayal so as to provide particularly Ninja-like guidance.

KŌSEI KIRIGAKURE-GATA

攻勢霧隠れ型

Metsubushi destroy not merely the opponents' vision but also their volition, their will to fight.

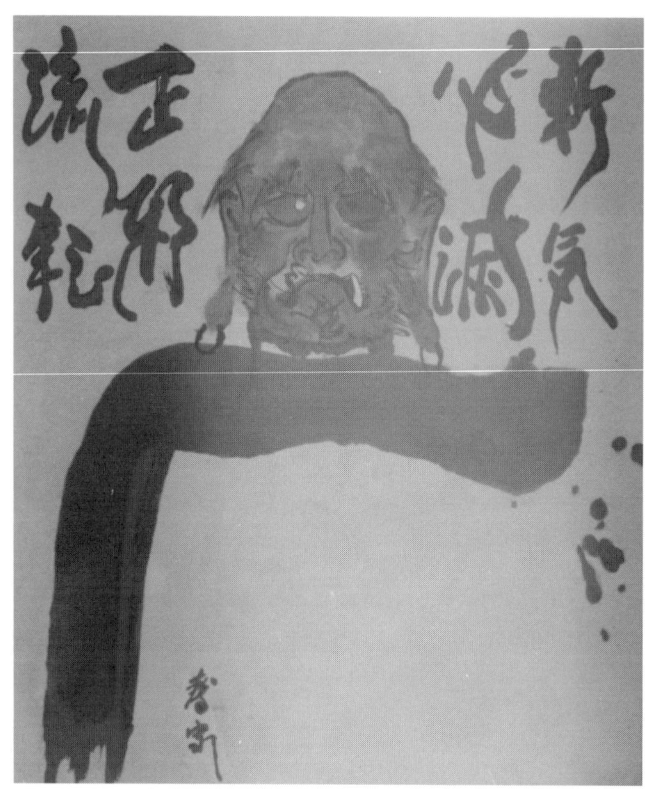

Zanki Hitsumetsu, Seija Ruten: good and evil are constantly in flux —those who think of the sword, die by the sword

Chapter

6

The infinite variety of Ninpō Taijutsu

千変兆化・忍法体術

NINPŌ TAIJUTSU EMBODIES THE VITALITY OF MANKIND

I suspect that the reason so many people throughout the world are interested in Ninpō Taijutsu is that they can sense the human life-force within it. In a sense, it is like the tantra. Ninjutsu has the power to strengthen life force, and, conversely, to constrain life force. It serves both functions, and on occasion may exert its power through a combination of the two.

Miyamoto Musashi's *Book of Five Rings*, written in 1645, is divided into five volumes: Earth, Water, Fire, Wind, Void. Another, older Japanese document contains a volume entitled "Shinden Kohyō no Hikan"("Secret scroll of the divine tradition of tigers' transformation"), with five entries describing Kamae or fighting attitudes: the Crouching Tiger, Raging Tiger, Starving Tiger, Nursing Tiger, and Thundering Tiger.

The Crouching Tiger Kamae is a form where you lie quietly, watching the movements of the enemy forces with sharp eyes, then suddenly change into a fierce tiger to fight.

The Raging Tiger Kamae is the form of a fierce tiger who whips up a wind and fights.

The Starving Tiger Kamae is a terrifying form, in which you fight in Sutemi, the spirit of self-sacrifice: it is a question of 'eat or be eaten.'

The Nursing Tiger Kamae is a desperate form, used when your intention is to protect others at any cost.

The Thundering Tiger Kamae is like a bombardment of thunder and rain when faced with a strong enemy.

These are collectively known as "Koteki Ryōda (dragons and tigers fighting) Juppō Sesshō no Jutsu," and are the original forms of the Kata found in Budō. The "Ryūko no Maki" (dragon and tiger scrolls) are a later derivation.

The Dragon Scroll describes all things leading up to certain victory. The Tiger Scroll, in contrast, describes what one needs to know about various phenomena, objects, and people, as well as things one needs to predict, sense, and see through. In other words, the combination of the two great elements of the Dragon and the Tiger, having foresight and being certain of victory, is seen to be an important aspect of Budō. Martial artists who cannot develop this natural ability to predict, sense, and see through things

will never achieve the proverbial "100 victories in 100 fights," let alone "100 lives in 100 lights" (i.e. gaining enlightenment in each existence).

THE ESSENCE OF BUDŌ

The techniques of Budō are all highly polished masterpieces. However, if you 'learn' or memorize them, everything stops: you end up feeling trapped, and it has the opposite effect from that intended. Once you have learned a technique, you need to forget it. If you remember and recall it, it loses its authenticity. Learning a technique is not an end in itself, it merely indicates where you need to start. It is only by discarding memorized techniques, stripping them down, that you can discover a way forward to the next masterpiece.

In genuine Budō, any conventional 'common sense' about martial arts (fighting) that you might have learned in the past can actually get in the way. This is because common sense prevents you from changing. In real life, people who live beyond the bounds of common sense attack you suddenly, with scant regard for any rules of combat. You can hardly call yourself a martial artist if this throws you off balance.

The history of combat also demonstrates that only one out of every forty-eight great victories was won by regular (or 'frontal') attacks. As a Budōka might say, the other forty-seven were 'unnatural' forms which broke the mold. But the martial arts are unnatural in this way, they do lie outside the limits of conventional wisdom at any given time. The 'common sense' of the past should be recognized as an adulteration which needs to be removed; you should always take up the challenge of the new. Start learning from zero, and there is no end to the number of techniques that will emerge.

Incidentally, research into 280 of the most famous or representative battles from Ancient Greece onwards shows that a whole 274 were won by ambush or other forms of unconventional warfare! In other words, in only six cases was victory obtained by 'proper' methods.

Above all, it is important to maintain equanimity. You should be able to change any part of your life quite normally and naturally, just as your heart beats. Otherwise, you will end up stuck in your ways and unable to make your way through the world. In the martial arts, it is important to discard obsessive ideas, leave behind any adherence to forms, and abandon conventional common sense. By doing this your spirit will become more flexible, your 'capacity' as a martial artist will grow, those around you will acknowledge your preeminence, and you will be able to produce free, ever-changing techniques wherever and whenever you choose.

An old poem says, "Water's custom is to flow to low ground; yet here starts its journey up." Normally, water does flow from high places to lower ones: so says the 'received wisdom.' However, a martial artist would not agree at all. Rain becomes water vapor, rises into the skies, turns into clouds, and then becomes rain again, or a heat haze. Turning and turning, it is in a perpetual, cyclical motion. Ninja can use each phase sepa-

rately, as Suiton no Jutsu, Kasumi no Jutsu ('mist arts'), and the like. One can also perform Uton no Jutsu ('rain evasion') using cigarette smoke.

Sesshū (1420–1506), the great Suiboku (ink painting) and Sansui-ga (landscape) artist, and Yokoyama Taikan (1868–1958), an equally well-known Japanese painter, left us works of almost divine inspiration which take this perpetual motion of life as their theme. As it happens, the perpetual motion of life is also one of the secrets described in the Ninjutsu scrolls.

If we study Ninpō Taijutsu correctly, we naturally pick up various nuggets of wisdom about dealing with life in society. I certainly do not mean to imply that Ninpō Taijutsu is the sole, supreme way. Throughout history, all sorts of people had their own Taijutsu, be it the Taijutsu of farmers, the Taijutsu of merchants, or whatever. In modern times too, system engineers, photographers, stewardesses—each profession has developed its own appropriate type of Taijutsu. I am sure that those who continue training unremittingly, experience the greatest joy when they discover the heart of their chosen path from Taijutsu that they were unable to perform before.

Miyamoto Musashi (1584?–1645) is famous worldwide as a great swordsman. Despite having over sixty fights in his life, Musashi never lost. He is also said to be the founder of Niten Ichi-ryū, an unusual school of swordsmanship employing two swords. What many people do not know about Musashi is that he had also mastered a unique school of Taijutsu, Musashi-ryū. In his duel at Ganryūjima against the powerful opponent Sasaki Kojirō, he did not in fact hold a sword in each hand: instead he presented a long, wooden sword. Faced with Kojirō, who allegedly had a sword as long as a washing pole and was highly skilled at handling it, Musashi leapt up, swung his wooden sword down, struck the top of Sasaki's head and thereby decided the match. The secret of Musashi's strength, in this match too, did not in fact lie in his Two-Sword School but in his Taijutsu. This school of Taijutsu was still passed down until the end of the Meiji period, and Takamatsu Sensei told me that he was once pitted against the man who had inherited leadership of the school.

One cannot use weapons if one is ignorant of Taijutsu. It is probably no exaggeration to say that it is because the Japanese "martial arts" forgot Taijutsu that they ended up as sports, departing from the path of the true martial ways.

Many people believe they have understood what Musashi was really like by reading *Musashi*, the wonderful book by Yoshikawa Eiji that was translated by my late friend Charles S. Terry. Yoshikawa Eiji (1892–1962) was such a good novelist that the conventional image of Musashi has been greatly influenced by his work. But Yoshikawa Eiji's book and the real Miyamoto Musashi are two separate entities. If one reads the famous *Book of Five Rings*, which Musashi wrote for the sake of his students and future generations, completing it just one week before his death, one encounters many views and thoughts that evidently stem from a desire to win. This literary effort took him approximately two years. They must have been burdensome years. Like Christ, Musashi carried a cross: in his case, that of being a Bushi. To discover the true Musashi, one needs to interpret him from a viewpoint far removed from Yoshikawa Eiji's work.

Miyamoto Musashi certainly understood the principles of combat well. However, I think he had a lonely life (in the Wabi-Sabi sense). It is a known fact that in his later years he devoted himself to painting, in order to banish this loneliness. Musashi also claimed in his twenty-one-article "Dokkōdō" ("The Solitary Way") to "respect both Buddha and Kami, but rely on neither," yet I wonder if Musashi really had this awareness. "Dokkōdō" and the *Book of Five Rings*, which he wrote while practicing Zen under the guidance of the monk Shunzan, show a distinct bias towards Buddhist interpretations.

When I first went abroad, it was August. I announced to the people I met in New York, "I have no country. I am not Japanese. I am UFO." By "UFO" I did not mean an unidentified flying object. Twenty-one years later, these words have become reality; now in August 2003, the true nature of this UFO can be revealed. What I meant was "Unusual Friends Okay," in the sense that no matter how weird or extreme a person might seem, I still welcome them as my friend.

Bujinden, main training hall of the Bujinkan

SHINOBI SIX-FOOT STAFF VERSUS SWORD

忍びの六尺棒と刀

Faced with an opponent in Seigan no Kamae, sweep away his sword, then knock him down, using the six-foot staff to control his neck.

Shinobi six-foot staffs include a wide range of gadgets or tricks. Some, for example, incorporate tubes like paper 'cups' containing weapons or explosives.

KYOGETSU SHŌGE VERSUS SWORD

距跋渉毛と刀

Kyogetsu Shōge (see p. 45) can be used to entwine the opponent, apply locks, disarm him, and tie him up within a space that is both physical and mental, before you disappear through Tongyō.

KATATE-NUKI: ONE-HANDED DRAW

片手抜き

As the opponent begins to cut in from Jōdan, draw your sword with one hand and meet him halfway, then continue to cut, with your energy as much as with the blade itself. It is important to have sufficient mettle to handle his Jōdan as merely a joke (also "Jōdan").

The so-called 'mystical' techniques for immobilizing an opponent at a distance, such as Tō-ate and Fudō Kanashibari, truly come to life at times like this.

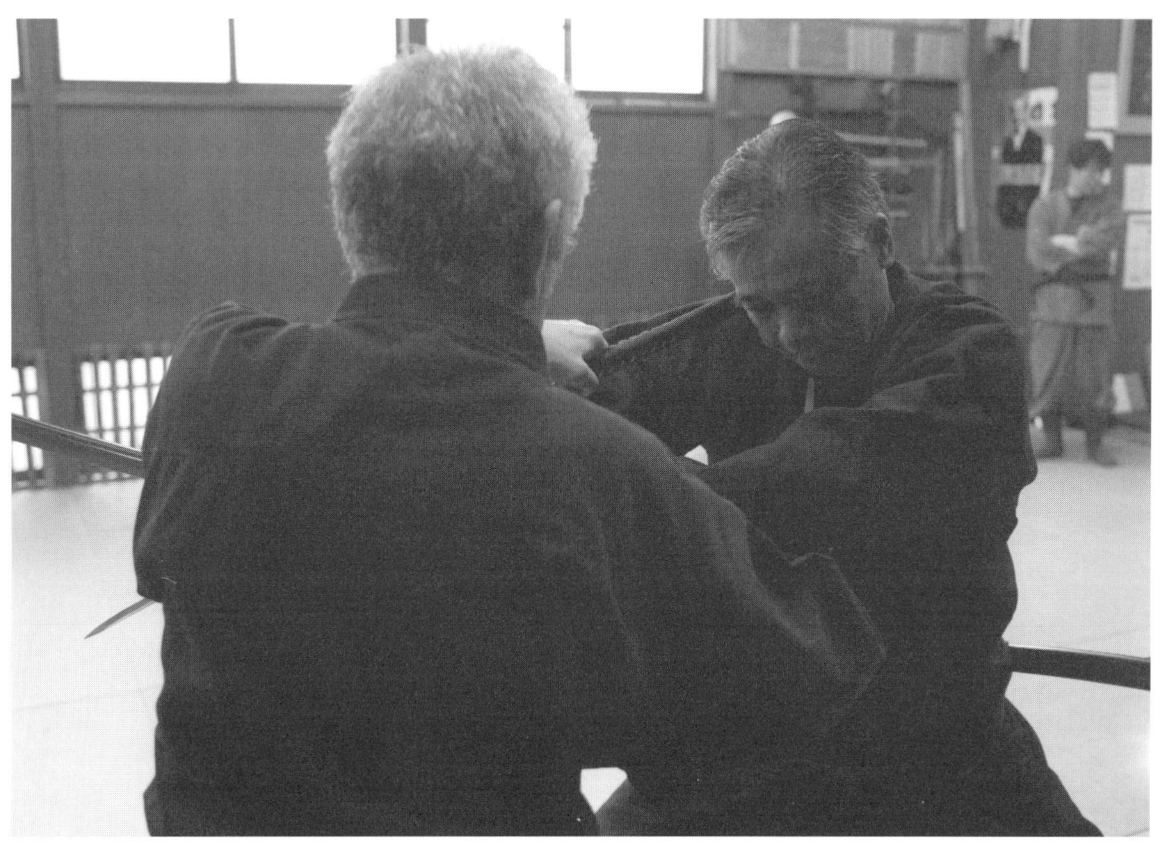

KAGE NO ITTŌ: SHADOW SWORD

影の一刀

As the opponent comes in to cut from Daijōdan, you draw the sword hidden behind your back, sweep his attack aside with the force of your intention rather than just the sword, and cut in. The elegance of this move is similar to that found in Japanese paintings featuring the traditional themes of nature: snow, moon, and flowers.

MUTŌ-DORI (ONE AGAINST ONE)

無刀捕り（一人対一人）

The principle of Mutō-dori should be learned naturally, without either you or the enemy wearing a sword.

MUTŌ-DORI (ONE AGAINST TWO): VERSION I

無刀捕り（一人対一二人）その一

NINJA GARDENERS

Claude Monet (1840–1926), the foremost French Impressionist, is known to have been quite overwhelmed by Japanese Ukiyo-e woodblock prints, and to have created a Japanese garden at his house. Seeing the beauty of light and shadow reflected on the water surface, he painted his well-known pictures of water lilies. Japanese gardens use water, rocks, plants, and scenic objects (such as stone lanterns) to create a space at one with the boundless beauty of nature. It is indeed a world of dark, unfocused elegance. Japanese gardens were always deep and somewhat esoteric in this way.

Kobori Enshū (1579–1647), the gardener who was renowned for creating the Katsura Detached Palace, commonly regarded to be the greatest Japanese garden, was also a landscape gardener, tea expert, and military commander, living at the beginning of the Edo period. He was highly skilled at painting, calligraphy, and Waka poetry. He further demonstrated his natural talents when working as the public works commissioner for Sunpu Castle, Fushimi Castle, Osaka Castle, and Nijō Castle. Gardens in the castles and mansions of contemporary Daimyō (feudal lords) were creations which combined practicality with great artistic sense, and also functioned as symbols of power. Hence, by looking at the garden of a castle or a Daimyō's mansion, you could read from it how cultured the owner was and how much power or wealth they possessed. Because of this, many of the "Oniwa-ban" who looked after the gardens were not simple garden-keepers, but people of great character and insight, who excelled at divination and Feng Shui/Dunjia. Saigō Takamori (1827–77), the hero active from the end of the Edo period to the Meiji restoration who is mentioned in Uchimura Kanzō's *Representative Men of Japan*, progressed from an Oniwa-ban employed by Shimazu Nariakira, Daimyō of the Shimazu domain, to domain leader, then a leader of Japan itself.

MUTŌ-DORI (ONE AGAINST TWO): VERSION 2

無刀捕り（一人対二人）その二

MUTŌ-DORI (ONE AGAINST TWO): VERSION 3

無刀捕り（一人対二人）その三

MUTŌ-DORI (ONE AGAINST THREE)

無刀捕り（一人対三人）

KANGI: LEVERAGE TECHNIQUES

槓技

Few people have been taught the Kasumi no Den ("message of the mist") known as Shinbō ("true, enduring stick"). You project a shadow image of yourself into the void.

TRANSCENDING GOOD AND BAD IN LITERARY AND MILITARY ARTS

Takamatsu Sensei left many wonderful paintings of dragons and the like. I too enjoy creating calligraphy and drawing "Giga," capricious sketches (I actually use a play on words, and refer to mine using different characters, as merely 'artificial grace'). I would not be able to produce such paintings or calligraphy if I did not train in the martial arts. It is only because of my understanding of the martial arts that internal features naturally rise to the surface. With normal painters this does not happen, because it is not a question of technical aptitude, or anything along the lines of their 'touch.' Takamatsu Sensei once praised my artistic efforts, and I therefore tried studying Western-style painting, Japanese-style painting, abstract painting, and Indian ink painting. Now, however, if someone places paper in front of me, I take my brush in my hand and simply drop ink onto the page in whatever way feels right. If the result does not seem that good, I leave it for a while, then add things or amend it. It is all done quite spontaneously. Earlier I mentioned the saying, "Budōka should be neither strong nor weak, neither soft nor hard." With painting too, whether one is good or bad is immaterial. The essence of art lies in a realm beyond such petty concerns. When painting, I always try to retain a sense of painting both the front and back (the Omote and Ura) of the subject, and keep in mind a desire to make the world a better place through my art.

BISENTŌ: BROW BLADE

眉尖刀

The Bisentō is the original form of the halberd. It is said that when Kannon rides a dragon through the clouds, her brow sucks in evil demons. This is paralleled by the name and shape of the Bisentō, which itself slices through space, through the floating world, just as if dismembering demons from within a cloud.

TRANSLATOR'S NOTE

As one might expect from a Ninja, Dr. Hatsumi moves and writes in a type of 'mist' where nothing is allowed to be too clear. His art—whether his movements or his writing—should be felt rather than understood. His written vocabulary, just as his vocabulary of martial moves, is unconventional to say the least, and the meaning of the words he uses is often less important than their sound and the implications thereof. All of this places him in direct opposition to his translator, whose mission is (normally) to convey the original meaning as accurately and clearly as possible.

Clarifying unintentional ambiguities is part of a translator's daily life. However, transferring words which are deliberately phrased as phonetic puns so as to have two—or indeed, many more—meanings into another language, while yet retaining as much as possible of all of these different senses, is nigh on impossible. Sōke makes frequent use of such triple entendres, as tools to cut his readers free from conventional modes of thought. The 'secret techniques' of this book are secret as much because of the way they are written as anything else; and the true techniques are not the moves shown in the photos but the principles hidden inside the text.

It was therefore a great relief when on 29 October 2003 Sōke instructed me to translate only my "image" of this book, adapting the text based on my interpretation of his art. Of course, the result is halfway between the two. I have tried to retain at least sufficient ambiguity to allow readers to "imagine" their own subtexts. If some sentences can be read two or more ways, that is quite intentional. I have, however, had to simplify and amplify the text in many places, and am profoundly grateful to Chris 'Akshara' Reynolds for his advice on this point. For those who are interested in the details, there is unfortunately no alternative but to read this work in the original Japanese—as Sōke has also said, his martial arts can only truly be conveyed in Japanese.

Sōke requires his students to read between the lines, to see the hidden ("Hiden") truths between the pictures, and to understand above all that nothing is fixed. If you notice that some of the descriptions do not match the photographs, that is no oversight: it is an intentional effort to help widen your perceptions. Many Japanese terms have been retained through necessity, although brief explanations have been provided in the glossary. In some cases, however, the only explanation available is a "Kuden" from one who knows.

One final note: although the readings of Japanese names are equally ambiguous, and none should be taken as entirely definitive, they have at least been written in the conventional Japanese order, i.e. with the family name first.

Ben Jones

GLOSSARY

There are many Japanese terms which are essential to an understanding of the martial arts, and for which adequate English versions do not or cannot exist. The glossary below is designed to help those with little knowledge of the Bujinkan arts read the main text. However, some of the concepts are so deep that I thought it best to limit the glossary to literal translations: additional interpretation is up to the reader. A few names of techniques etc. have been omitted as non-essential to an understanding of the text.

Aruki = Walk

Bō = Stick, especially six-foot staff
Budō/Bufū/Bujutsu = Martial arts
Budōka/Bugeisha = Martial artist
Bujinkan = Dr. Hatsumi's training group
Bushi = Samurai
Bushidō = Way of the warrior

Daijōdan = High sword stance
Daitō = Long sword (Katana or Tachi)
Densho = Written transmission
Dōjō = Place for training in the arts

Edo = (period) 1600–1868; also old name for Tōkyō

Geta = Clogs
Gyaku = Reverse; also joint lock

Hanbō = Three-foot staff
Hi = Secret; Hiden = secret transmission
Hichō = Flying bird

Jū = Ten, or ten syllables (Jūji)
Jū = soft (different Kanji); e.g., Jū-tai-jutsu
Juppō Sesshō = Contact in ten directions
Jutsu = Techniques

Kaeri/Gaeri = Return
Kamae = Stance
Kata/Gata = Form
Koppō = Bone arts; or finer points of an art
Kosshi = Bones & fingers
Kote = Wrist

Ku = Nine; Kuji = nine syllables (used in spells)
Kuden = Oral transmission
Kusarigama = Chain and sickle
Kyo & Jitsu = Falsehood & Truth
Kyūsho = Painful spot

Makimono = Scroll
Metsubushi = Blinding powder

Nagare = Flow
Nage = Throw
Nin/Shinobi = Perseverance; also subterfuge
Ninja/Shinobi [no Mono] = Person who does Nin
Ninjutsu/Ninpō = The techniques/ways of Nin
(often used interchangeably with Taijutsu/Budō)

Omote & Ura = Front & back

Ryū = School or style of martial arts

Sanshin = Three hearts, or heart of three
Senban = Type of Shuriken
Sensei = Teacher
Shuriken = Throwing blades
Sōke = Head of the school
Suigetsu = Solar plexus

Tabi = Split-toed footwear
Tai = Body (Tai-jutsu = body techniques)
Ten Chi Jin = Heaven Earth Man
Tengu = Mythical winged creature
Tobi = Jump
Togakure = One of the 9 Ryū, from Mt. Togakushi
Ton = Escape; also the "Dun" in Dunjia divination
Tori/Dori = Take; also bird

Uke = Receive

Yoko = Side